Steve Murray has brought Reiki to those who can't afford to spend the big bucks for spiritual lessons/meditations and healing. (Hey, didn't Christ do that?) I believe in Reiki and I believe that the here and now IS the here and now. Steve Murray is right on about channeling energy through the distance, we are one, we are connected, whether we think good or evil, we are all connected so it makes sense that you would be able to send energy this way. We all have the spiritual potential to heal others and saying so and making it easily accessible puts Steve Murray high on my list. Reiki Master and Ethical Master is what I say. *BL*

I bought Steve's 3 books and 4 DVDs (level 1, level 2, master, and psychic attunements) and loved them. The attunements are at least as powerful as the in-person one I had and I am VERY sensitive to energy. After Steve's attunements and books I have a definite "feeling the flow" of Reiki every time I invoke the power. Steve's books made so much more sense than the "traditional" school to a healer like myself. It is obvious he really understands the energy he works with and the true power of intention. *EO*

I have tried the love issues attunement twice. Once, I did it myself and the other time my husband attuned me. Both times I received great results. I am very pleased as I have long term problems regarding giving and receiving love. I notice a difference in me and my husband does as well. I plan on doing more attunements and some chakra work (Steve's 2nd book will come in handy!) to further my progress. This book is by far the most valuable book in my collection. Thanks, Steve, for writing such a great book. *LM*

I have always wanted to take Reiki classes. It was something stronger than I was pushing me to it. One time I told a friend about my feeling. She told me I could not because I was poor and this course I asked for cost too much. I prayed to God without telling anyone. If He wanted, I would be one master Reiki. Now, with your DVD and books I found out I have been a Reiki Master all my life. I thank you, Master Steve, for opening me to the calling of myself. *IN*

My fondest appreciation and thanks for the most comprehensive, profound, and beautiful information you have imparted about Reiki in the trilogy of books, DVDs and music attunements I received from you. I had wanted to become a Reiki Master, but the $5,000-$10,000 fee was quite prohibitive for me. Thanks to you, I was able to finally realize my dream. It was really precious reviewing Levels 1, 2, and 3 and finally being blessed with your Reiki Master Attunement on that very special day. *LS*

I'm a newcomer to Reiki and feel so blessed that I found you. Your Healing and Psychic Attunements are beyond words. The power is so profound that already (even after two days) I'm experiencing releases and enhancement. The synchronicity of the universe never ceases to amaze me. I've become aware of the need to "recapitulate" (as per Carlos Castaneda), but had no idea how to release all this crap that's been surfacing (that I fantasized had been let go a long time ago). Now, I've found the key in your Attunements. *JM*

I just wanted to let you know how wonderfully powerful and healing your Aura Attunement has been for both my husband and me. For me, after doing an intention on eliminating a habit that I have, I had a dream that gave me divine information that I would never have expected. The results of this dream removed so much past untruths and bogus beliefs that I am truly amazed. It is as though my whole spiritual world has expanded. After doing an attunement on my husband for fear, he too was made aware of a past childhood experience that had a long-term negative effect on him. We are so grateful.... thank you. *CK*

In Vol. 2, Steve only focused on affecting physical ailments within the body. These attunements can be carried out in 15 to 20 minutes because they are so well pinpointed upon the condition. I tried one on myself for anger issues that had been affecting me for two days, and was pleasantly surprised that my emotions and (at times) extreme states stabilized within the hour and I am feeling continually better as time goes on. Excellent! *CC*

Reiki False Beliefs
Exposed for All
Misinformation
Kept Secret By A Few
Revealed

Steve Murray

First Printing

Body & Mind Productions, Inc.

Reiki False Beliefs
Exposed for All
Misinformation
Kept Secret By A Few
Revealed

Published by
Body & Mind Productions
820 Bow Creek Lane, Las Vegas, NV 89134
Website: www.healingreiki.com
Email: bodymindheal@aol.com

First Printing October 2006

Library of Congress Cataloging-in-Publication Data
Murray, Steve
Reiki False Beliefs Exposed for All Misinformation Kept
Secret By A Few Revealed
/ Murray, Steve – 1st ed.
Library of Congress Control Number 2006903402
ISBN # 0-9771609-6-3
Includes bibliographical references and index.
1. Reiki 2. New Age 3.Alternative Health
4. Self-Healing 5. Spiritual 6. Healing

Cover design: Dan Berger @ foxtrot2112@yahoo.com
Type design, production: Dan Berger
Editors: Sonya Baity, Carol von Raesfeld
Drawings: Lisa Gauvain

DVDs-CDs-BOOKS

BOOKS by STEVE MURRAY

Reiki The Ultimate Guide
Learn Sacred Symbols and Attunements
Plus Reiki Secrets You Should Know

Reiki The Ultimate Guide Vol. 2
Learn Reiki Healing with Chakras
plus New Reiki Healing Attunements
for All Levels

Reiki The Ultimate Guide Vol. 3
Learn New Reiki Aura Attunements
Heal Mental and Emotional Issues

Cancer Guided Imagery Program
For Radiation, Chemotherapy, Surgery
and Recovery

Reiki False Beliefs Exposed for All
Misinformation Kept Secret By A
Few Revealed

Stop Eating Junk!
In 5 Minutes a Day for 21 Days

DVDS by STEVE MURRAY

Reiki Master Attunement
Become a Reiki Master

Reiki 1st Level Attunement
Give Healing Energy to Yourself
and Others

Reiki 2nd Level Attunement
Learn and Use the Reiki Sacred
Symbols

Reiki Psychic Attunement
Open and Expand Your Psychic
Abilities

Reiki Healing Attunement
Heal Emotional-Mental Physical-
Spiritual Issues

Lose Fat and Weight
Stop Eating Junk!
In 5 Minutes a Day for 21 Days

Cancer Guided Imagery
Program for Radiation

Cancer Guided Imagery
Program for Chemotherapy

Cancer Guided Imagery
Program for Surgery

30-Day Subliminal
Weight Loss Program

Pain Relief Using Your
Unconscious Mind
A Subliminal Program

Fear & Stress Relief
Using Your Unconscious Mind
A Subliminal Program

Stop Smoking Using Your Unconscious Mind
A Subliminal Program

5

CDs *by STEVE MURRAY*

Reiki Healing Music
Attunement: Volume One

Reiki Healing Music
Attunement: Volume Two

Reiki Psychic Music
Attunement: Volume One

Reiki Psychic Music
Attunement: Volume Two

Cancer Fear & Stress Relief Program
Reduce Fear and Stress During Cancer
Treatment and Recovery

DVDs *by BODY & MIND PRODUCTIONS*

Learning to Read the Tarot
Intuitively

Learning to Read the Symbolism
of the Tarot

This book is dedicated to

All my Reiki students worldwide

Foreword

I hope this book will enlighten all who read it. Or at the very least, plant the seed of the possibility of utilizing different Reiki healing options in minds with the intent the seed will sprout in the near future.

Steve Murray

CONTENTS

A lengthy waiting period is needed before receiving
    the next level Attunement
Reiki Attunements should be kept secret
Reiki Long Distance Attunements do not work
Free Reiki Attunements are free
A Reiki Attunement is needed to become a healer
A special power is transferred during a Reiki
    Level Attunement
You should not repeat the same Reiki Attunement
The eyes need to be closed when receiving a
    Reiki Attunement
Intent is not needed when giving a Reiki Attunement
A new Reiki Attunement cancels previous Attunements

Reiki Healers do not get sick
All Reiki Healers have the same healing ability
A Reiki Healer needs to have hot hands
A Reiki Healer lives a shorter physical life
A Reiki Healer cannot take on the symptoms
    of the client
You do not have to practice Reiki
A person needs to be a Buddhist to become
    a Reiki Healer
A Reiki Healer must be vegetarian
Reiki Healers can lose their healing ability
A Reiki Healer should be healed before giving Reiki to others

$10,000 is the fee to become an authentic Reiki Master
Reiki Masters are Spiritual Masters
Reiki Grand Masters are special
Independent Reiki Masters are not true Reiki Masters
Reiki Masters are responsible for miracles
It takes years to become a Reiki Master
All Reiki Masters are teachers
Reiki Masters cannot give Attunements without
    Reiki Symbols

13

Where I let go of what I am, I become what I might be.

- Lao Tzu

Introduction

Years ago, I started sending Reiki Long Distance Attunements to my students around the world through videotaped programs. I am pleased to say the people I have attuned through my programs have integrated Reiki into their daily lives and are now healing themselves and others. They are making a difference in the world and helping to achieve my Reiki Mission:

To make Reiki knowledge, guidance and Attunements available to everyone that seeks them. To make Reiki 1st, 2nd and Master Level Attunements affordable for everyone, so healing can be spread throughout the world.

Although extremely successful, my method of attuning students to Reiki through video was initially frowned upon in some Reiki circles. In my book, Reiki The Ultimate Guide, the first in my trilogy, I wrote about that early resistance to my attuning method.

The beliefs about Reiki Long Distance Attunements have dramatically evolved since I released my first Reiki Attunement videos. They have now become widely accepted by the majority of the Reiki community. Reiki books that are being published today acknowledge the effectiveness of Reiki Long Distance Attunements. In fact, a large majority of all new Reiki Healers receive their Reiki Attunements long distance and this is one of the reasons why Reiki is rapidly spreading around the world.

Through my programs, I have attuned tens of thousands of people around the world to Reiki and that number continues to grow daily. The reason I know that I have attuned such a large number of people is simple: I know the quantity of Reiki Attunement videos and DVDs that I have replicated over the years for my distributors and my web site. The numbers of Reiki Attunements are most likely double what I quote because one program is usually used to attune family members, friends and fellow students. The programs are even rented and borrowed from libraries. I continue to replicate DVDs to keep up with the worldwide demand.

Why am I telling you about the number of people I have attuned to Reiki? It's because they are the main reason this book was written. I receive questions about Reiki from my students via e-mail, telephone, and letters every day. Most of the time, the questions raised in these communications are similar — concerns about conflicting Reiki information they have read or heard, and they don't know what to believe or how to proceed. These questions also reflect confusion about different Reiki Symbols and Attunements, which may be different from the ones I teach. Also, my students are curious and puzzled about all the different branches, systems and schools of Reiki with different Reiki names that seem to keep surfacing around the world. This book addresses all of these concerns and more. Even though my primary incentive for writing this book was for my students, the information in the book can help and inform all Healers.

I know some of the writing in this book might be controversial, as in all my Reiki books, particularly the first one[1]. Segments of it may upset and offend some Reiki Healers and Reiki schools. One of the reasons they may be upset is they have a vested interest, either personal or business (financial), in a number of the Reiki false beliefs I expose. This group of Healers also may be offended because they believe it is sacrilegious to reveal Reiki Symbols and

---

[1] *Reiki The Ultimate Guide: Learn Sacred Symbols & Attunements plus Reiki Secrets You Should Know*

to explain how different Reiki Attunements are performed. However, what this select group thinks does not concern me because they are not in concurrence with my Reiki Mission Statement. As I stated, I wrote this book for my students around the world and all Healers who are open to the information I share. Nevertheless, I do ask that all who read it be guided by this quotation from Buddha:

"Believe nothing, no matter where you read it, or who said it, no matter if I have said it, unless it agrees with your own reason and your own common sense."

If you do not change directions, you may end up where you are heading.

- Lao Tzu

He who controls others may be powerful, but he who has mastered himself is mightier still.

- Lao Tzu

False Beliefs

TWO

Myth = Belief

Webster's Third New International Dictionary, Unabridged, defines "myth" as a story or belief, usually fanciful and imaginative that explains a natural phenomenon, social practice, or institution. A myth can also be used to designate a belief commonly held to be true, but utterly without factual basis. The same dictionary defines "belief" as something believed, a statement or body of statements held by the advocates of any class of views. So with Webster's definitions in mind, I believe what starts out as a Reiki Myth metamorphoses into a Reiki False Belief.

Reiki False Beliefs

Over the years, Reiki has accumulated a number of widespread false beliefs concerning what the Reiki Healer cannot or should not do when using Reiki in various situations. There are also many false beliefs that put limitations and restrictions on Reiki itself and abundant false beliefs pertaining to its history.

The origins of most Reiki false beliefs are unknown, but like an urban legend, once one is started, it seems to take on a life of its own. I suspect that some false beliefs originated from a Reiki Healer's good intentions to warn others of a bad experience that happened as a coincidence when they were using Reiki at a particular time. They mistakenly linked the use of Reiki to their own personal circumstances and karma when it had nothing to do with Reiki.

I am sure some false beliefs were constructed by a Reiki Master's self-serving motive. For example, one false belief is that Reiki Long Distance Attunements do not work[2], so one needs an Attunement and/or needs to take a class in person (given, of course, by the Reiki Healer who is perpetuating

---

[2] False belief explained in Chapter 10

that false belief). Some false beliefs are attributable to simple ignorance, without thought or common sense as to what information is being spread.

I do know most of the false beliefs about Reiki history have been linked directly to Hawayo Takata, who is credited with bringing Reiki from Japan to the West in 1938. I don't know why she spread the false beliefs (nobody really does, and if they claim they do, it's just hearsay). I can only speculate that she spread the myths that eventually became false beliefs to make Reiki more widely accepted in America, and by doing so, she gave Reiki a larger-than-life history.

This is "old news" today in view of the fact that many new Reiki books[3] have done a great job exposing these false beliefs. Unfortunately, however, even with all the information out there, select questions regarding a few false beliefs about Reiki history keep surfacing from new and experienced Reiki Healers. By exposing these false beliefs in this book, I hope to put an end to them once and for all.

We should not be concerned about how these false beliefs started. The challenge is in stopping them from being passed on in Reiki classes, through word of mouth, on the Internet and in books. New Reiki Healers (and even some experienced ones) take these false beliefs at face value and never question them, which could cause harm to themselves and others by not receiving or giving Reiki in certain situations. The bottom line is that the proliferation of these false beliefs hurts the growth and spread of Reiki and confuses Reiki Healers.

---

[3] I have listed a few in the bibliography.

Letting Go

I understand that letting go of any false beliefs regarding Reiki might be difficult, especially if one has held some of these beliefs for years. Some of the false beliefs may have been taught to you when you first became a Reiki Healer, so naturally you assumed they were true.

All I ask is that you keep an open mind and use your intuition when reading a false belief about Reiki. If you find yourself disagreeing with part or even all of what I say, don't worry about it or dwell on it, just read on, particularly if you experience an emotional charge[4] when you read it. If that happens, what I suggest you do is re-read the false belief(s) after you have finished the book, then close your eyes and see if you still disagree with all or part of what I say on an intuitive level. What will likely happen is that in the time which elapses between when you first read the false belief(s) and when you re-read it, your psychic ability, intuitiveness, and common sense will enable you to change your feelings about it. If your feelings remain the same, then hang onto any and all beliefs you deem to be true - it's your prerogative.

---

[4] It's a strong emotional reaction (anger, fear, love, etc.) to something you see, read or hear.

Book Format

To keep things simple and easy to find and understand, I have categorized the false beliefs into chapters related to their topic. In each chapter, I state the Reiki false belief, then explain why it is false.

The words of truth are always paradoxical.

— Lao Tzu

Learning Reiki False Beliefs

THREE

Only one bona fide Reiki System to learn

The only time there was truly one Reiki System was when Mikao Usui[5] was teaching and using his system for healing. He named the Reiki System Usui Reiki Ryoho, which means the Usui method for spiritual healing.

---

[5] Person given credit for rediscovering Reiki in Japan during the late 1800s.

Actually, the whole process of evolving Reiki teachings and methods started after Hawayo Takata's[6] death in December of 1980. Several of the Reiki Masters she had taught began to alter the way they performed Reiki and how it was passed on to their students. Now, with the exponential growth of new and modified Reiki Systems (and the numbers keep growing!) there is really not just one bona fide Reiki System today.

In fact, there are so many different Reiki Systems[7] it can be very confusing for a person trying to decide on which Reiki System to learn. I teach the Usui System[8] because I believe it's the easiest to learn and perform, and the most effective way to use Reiki. I understand that the system I teach is a variation of Usui's original system - different teachers have modified it through the years before it was taught to me. I emphasize the ease to perform the Usui Reiki System that I teach in comparison to all the ritual[9] in many of the other Reiki Systems available today. Let me add, some people do enjoy in-depth, long ritual, and there is nothing wrong with that.

Problems and confusion arise when individuals and schools claim their Reiki System is the only bona fide system and is far superior, effective, or more powerful than other systems. Out of all the Reiki Systems now available, are all but one of them bona fide and the rest wrong? Of course not; that would be absurd and judgmental. All of these systems are producing healing results for Healers and their clients.

---

[6] Given credit for first teaching Reiki in the West.
[7] See Chapter 10 for more information.
[8] All my DVDs, CDs and books are based on Usui Reiki.
[9] See Chapter 10 for information on ritual in Reiki.

It is common for most Reiki teachers to put their own spin on the Reiki System they believe in and teach. A new Reiki System (or branch) is created when teachers change or modify what they have been taught and create a new name for the system (some even use their own personal name) and add the word "Reiki." Some even try and trademark the new name and/or the system they created (but most fail). I personally feel that applying for a trademark for any Reiki System is related to ego, money, and control, especially when the person's own name is used.

Since there is not just one Reiki System today, I suggest taking your time to look into the different systems of Reiki. One system may prove to be highly effective for one person while it might not be suited for another. The simple fact is, no matter what any person tells you, a Reiki System will work if the person using it believes in it. Just find a system that resonates with you and study it. It's the end result (healing) that really matters.

Only natural born Healers can learn Reiki

This is a common belief, that only natural Healers can learn Reiki. People from all walks of life, different cultures, young and old have become successful Reiki Healers. Many were never told or thought they were natural Healers.

The reality is we are all natural Healers with natural abilities to use our life force (Reiki) for healing. The challenge is, without a Reiki System, most people would lack guidance in using their natural healing ability for themselves and others. Reiki simply is a system (process) that uses your life force that's easy to learn and requires no previous training. As an added benefit to learning Reiki, one may find life and health altered for the best, altered in ways that were previously unimaginable. There may even be a development of a higher level of consciousness and spirituality to accompany and complement the other beneficial changes.

Reiki is difficult to learn

Reiki is not difficult, nor does it take a long time to learn. Learning Reiki is not dependent on one having any prior experience with healing, meditation or any other kind of previous training. As soon as students receive an Attunement, they have the ability to perform Reiki. After that, it's only a matter of practicing the teachings and techniques you have been taught or have access to.

This false belief is spread to make Reiki seem more of a challenge and give an air of mystery to the process of becoming a Healer. A few teachers do use this false belief for their own benefit by saying it takes months and even years to learn Reiki to keep you coming back to their classes. The majority of Reiki teachers do not use this tactic. They teach Reiki classes on a weekend with the Attunement. The class can be one or two days long and that's all you need to get started. Or they have teaching and Attunement programs similar to mine where you learn at your own pace and in your own space.

Reiki has to be taught in person

The belief that Reiki has to be taught in person is usually perpetuated by a Reiki Master's need to keep Reiki classes filled. This belief usually coincides with the belief that Reiki Attunements have to be given in person to work[10].

The truth of the matter is, classes are great if you can afford them, they are given close by, and you have the time to attend them. They are also good for interaction with your peers. Today, with all the print media, Internet information, chat room exchanges, Reiki forums, etc., that make Reiki teachings available, you have options. Just as you can receive an education in many subjects online or by correspondence (or a combination of both), it's the same with Reiki. You do not need to be taught in person anymore to learn Reiki. Of course, years ago when Reiki teachings were not accessible the way they are now, this was not a false belief.

I feel this turn of events is great because it gives people access to learning Reiki, when in the past, because of circumstances or money issues, many may not have been able to do so.

If you want to take a class, by all means, do so. Just keep an open mind to all other sources of Reiki teachings available that you can include in your healing and learning journey.

---

[10] See Chapter 10 for more information on this subject.

Higher fees guarantee quality Reiki teachings

Do not confuse high fees with quality when it comes to learning Reiki. People assume paying higher fees[11] guarantees informative Reiki teachings. Unfortunately, that's not always the case.

I hear stories from my students who have paid large sums for Reiki teachings in classes that can last up to several days; however, when I speak with them about what they learned, they have very little knowledge about Reiki and how to perform healing and Attunements on themselves and others.

I am not saying that you cannot get quality teachings from a Reiki Master who charges high fees, because you can. All I'm saying is there should be a clear reason why you are paying the additional money. For example, perhaps they may have additional teachings or techniques that you think are beneficial to learn which you cannot obtain elsewhere.

The simple solution is aspiring Reiki students must do their homework when selecting a Reiki Master Teacher. There are a large number of Reiki Masters who teach Reiki at reasonable fees and have quality teachings to choose from. When looking for a Reiki Master Teacher you need one with whom you feel comfortable. Look for one the same way you would look for any other professional.

---

[11] High fees are very subjective, but once you start comparing teaching fees, you will know what a high fee is when one is quoted to you.

Do your due diligence. Search the Internet and library, talk to friends for information on teachers.Interview your potential teachers. Find out their beliefs and experience, speak to their previous clients and students and compare their fees. Once you have done this, then decide.

Respond intelligently even to unintelligent treatment.
- Lao Tzu

False Beliefs on Receiving Reiki Treatments

FOUR

A Reiki Treatment must last an hour

At one time it was considered standard for a Reiki Healer to give a treatment by placing set hand positions on the body for 60 to 90 minutes or even longer. Lengthy treatments are no longer needed. Reiki has been evolving with new and faster methods for healing treatments for the mental, emotional, and physical body that take 15-20 minutes[12] and are just as effective.

There are a few obstacles that may arise as a result of lengthy treatments. Foremost, clients may become irritable and uncomfortable when channeled too much Reiki. Or they can grow tired or distracted during the treatment. The Healer giving such long treatments may also lose interest, experience muscle cramps, mental distraction or exhaustion.

These symptoms the Healer might experience could eventually lead to the Healer getting burned out and giving up the practice of Reiki. The world needs as many Healers as possible, so the drop-out rate of Reiki Healers must be kept to a minimum. Shorter, more effective Attunements help to achieve that goal.

With the correct Reiki Treatment and intent, a treatment should never last longer than half an hour. I personally believe 15-20 minutes is the best treatment time. It's all about the results, not the length of time.

Of course there are always exceptions to this and you will know intuitively when a session needs to be longer. However, I have found that if you are using the newer Reiki methods and techniques, this is very rare.

---

[12] *Reiki The Ultimate Guide,* Vols. 2 and 3 teach 15-20 minute healing Attunements in the Chakras and Aura for physical, mental, emotional, and spiritual issues.

Reiki Treatments are only
for sick people

Reiki is not just for people who are mentally, physically, or emotionally ill. It is also for people who are healthy and want to stay healthy. The challenge is that most people only discover or seek out Reiki when they are sick and most will stop using it when they become well. Once you become well you should continue to use Reiki. Through regular treatment and application it will promote balance for the body, the emotions and the mind (i.e., preventative medicine). Reiki Treatments will enhance the body's natural immune system, as well as help prevent lethargy and stress. Instead of waiting until illness manifests, use Reiki to promote your health as much as you can.

Regrettably, it is the human condition that all of us will experience ill health - physically, mentally, or emotionally at one time or another. The key to a healthy life while we are on our earthly journey is to use a balanced, holistic approach to healing and in every other aspect of our lives. Regular use of Reiki can be part of your holistic approach.

Jewelry should be removed during a
Reiki Treatment

Wearing jewelry when receiving a Reiki Treatment will not prevent and/or interfere with the flow of Reiki. Reiki can pass through anything (including jewelry), just as it can traverse time and space.

Reiki cannot be hindered; there is nothing that Reiki cannot penetrate, because as we already know, there is truly no solid matter...

The Healer should remove all jewelry or a watch before giving a Reiki Treatment. This is done not because it will interfere with the Reiki, but because a ticking watch and/or rattling jewelry can be a distraction and disrupts the peaceful atmosphere, especially when the Healer is working with the upper Chakras (around the head).

Legs and arms should not be crossed during a treatment

Having your legs and/or arms crossed when receiving a Reiki Treatment will not block or hinder the flow of Reiki, making the treatment less effective.

Reiki goes where the Healer's intent directs it to go and where the receiver needs it to go. Having your legs or arms crossed has nothing to do with intent, nor will it affect the flow of Reiki. There really isn't a position or posture that you can assume to make the treatment less effective or inaccessible. The position of the arms and legs of the person receiving Reiki is solely an individual preference based on what feels most comfortable, physically and emotionally.

Nudity is needed during a Reiki Treatment

I have been told there are several books and articles that recommend nude treatments, claiming they are required for stronger results or that certain areas of the body are easier to treat if one is unclothed. This is false.

I do know there are many stories on the Web and in Internet chat rooms about people falling victim to unethical Reiki Healers who ask them to remove their clothes before a treatment.

If you ever find yourself in a situation where a Reiki Healer tells you to remove your clothes, you should get up and leave immediately. Under no circumstance is there a need for either the Healer or the recipient of Reiki to remove clothing. Reiki can be channeled over long distance, to the past and future, so it can penetrate clothing. The removal of clothing is unnecessary and inappropriate.

Additionally, when receiving a treatment the hands of the Healer should never be placed on the breasts of women or on the genitals of any client.

The Healer should pay close attention to the client's level of comfort and personal boundaries during a Reiki Treatment. Loose fitting or comfortable clothing should be worn during a treatment and the removal of shoes and loosening of the belt can be done before receiving a treatment.

A Reiki Treatment can make you sick

A Reiki Treatment will not cause any harm. Regrettably, there are times that an illness gets worse before it gets better. When this occurs it is called a "healing crisis" and it takes place soon after a treatment or even during a treatment. A healing crisis does not manifest that often. A person who is unaware of the possibility of a healing crisis and has one, can mistakenly assume the Reiki Treatment has caused the sickness.

A healing crisis might only produce minor symptoms or they can be quite severe. The symptoms can include headache, stomachache or a general malaise. What is actually happening is the physical body is beginning the process of cleansing and healing. It does this by eliminating toxins that have accumulated from the illness. It is during this process that you might feel worse. The discomfort will usually only last for a few days. If the crisis lasts longer than three days, the person having the crisis should see a medical doctor.

21-days are required between Reiki Treatments

There can be a waiting period of a few days for a person to adjust to the Reiki Treatment, but 21 days is too long to wait for the next treatment if there is a physical illness or disease that needs to heal. Most Healers understand this and want you to come in for as many treatments as possible in the early stages of treatment.

This false belief does keep surfacing in the Reiki community. I can only guess the 21-day waiting period between treatments started from Takata's story of Usui. It's the story that Usui spent a total of 21 days in meditation by himself on Mt. Kurama before he was ready to come down. Somehow this was translated to the 21-day waiting period between treatments.

You must believe in Reiki for a treatment to work

Many Reiki Healers say that for a Reiki Treatment to be effective the client must believe in Reiki. Their thinking is, if a person does not believe in Reiki they will resist healing, whether at a conscious or a subconscious level. This is simply not true. A Reiki Treatment can help a person whether or not they believe in Reiki. This false belief has stopped Healers from giving Reiki Treatments to people who they feel do not believe in Reiki.

First of all, nobody should judge or make a determination regarding whether Reiki can or cannot help and then withhold Reiki Treatments based on that judgment. All Reiki Treatments will help on some level, be it physical, emotional, mental or spiritual. To what degree depends on the person receiving the treatment and their individual circumstances at the time they receive the treatment.

Just because a client does not exhibit any physical signs of healing right away, it doesn't mean healing is not taking place. Nor does it mean the subconscious mind did not want healing and blocked the Reiki.

What it does mean is that healing and changing is taking place in the Aura (emotional, mental, spiritual bodies) where the results cannot be seen until the healing resonates down to the physical body, which takes time. Of course, to what degree healing occurs depends on the person receiving the treatment and the individual circumstances at the time.

The bottom line is this, it is common for clients to be skeptical or not believe in Reiki because they can't see it. But, the majority of people want to believe in Reiki and its benefits and that's why they will try a Reiki Treatment. If a person is willing to receive Reiki, whatever their mindset about the Reiki Treatment, give the treatment and do not worry about making judgments about their conscious or subconscious mind.

Nature does not hurry, yet everything is accomplished.

- Lao Tzu

Great acts are made up of small deeds.

- Lao Tzu

False Beliefs on
Specific Reiki Treatments

Do not use Reiki on a person
with a pacemaker

It has been taught in Reiki classes that you should not treat
a client with a pacemaker. This false belief is made on the
wrong assumption that Reiki energy is electromagnetic or

has electromagnetic properties/characteristics, therefore, a Reiki Treatment will interfere with the proper functioning of the pacemaker and could short circuit the pacemaker and cause it to cease working. Some even go far as to say this belief only applies to analog pacemakers, not digital ones.

Reiki is not electromagnetic, nor does it have any similar attributes to it. If it did, you could measure Reiki by charging a wire with your hands, which would then create an electric current. A voltmeter would be able to detect the current. This has not yet happened, so do not let a pacemaker stop you from giving a Reiki Treatment.

Pregnant women should not receive Reiki Treatments

I am sure a majority of Healers have heard several versions of this false belief. One version is that women should not receive Reiki Treatments throughout their term because Reiki energy is too strong and would harm the unborn baby. The more specific version of the belief is that Reiki could cause a woman to miscarry within the first three months of her term because it would be too much for the unborn baby to process, but after that it is okay to use Reiki.

These two versions and any versions you may have heard are false and have no basis in fact. Reiki is your life force and will in no way cause loss of life.

I can only guess this belief was started years ago when a Reiki Healer was treating a woman who was in the early stages of her term, and during this time the woman unfortunately had a miscarriage, for whatever reason. The blame for the miscarriage was mistakenly directed towards the Reiki Treatment(s). I do believe Reiki Treatments have prevented miscarriages, although it never can be proven.

The truth is thousands of pregnant women have taken Reiki classes and received Reiki Attunements with beneficial results for the baby and themselves. Reiki has also been used during childbirth.

Reiki should not be used with surgical operations

The basis for this false belief is that Reiki may impact the potency of the anesthetic administered before an operation in one or two ways. The first way would have the patient not going under easily and requiring more toxic anesthesia. The second way would be the patient goes under easily, but then wakes up during the operation because not enough anesthesia was used. Both are false and without merit.

While giving Reiki before an operation may more likely cause less anesthetic to be needed, it also puts the patient in a state of relaxation, which may help make the operation, and certainly the recovery, more successful and expedient. As for the patient's waking up, the possibilities of that are remote and an anesthesiologist would quickly give more anesthetic. Even if that did happen, the benefits of Reiki far outweigh the brief awakening during an operation.

Reiki Treatments should not be given to diabetics

The foundation for this false belief is that a Reiki Treatment can instantly cure an insulin dependent diabetic, then they will go into shock and die from too much insulin. First of all, I would imagine if this happened to a diabetic (instant cure), they would have to be taking insulin at the same time they were receiving a Reiki Treatment, which would be most unusual. Miracles do happen with Reiki, but there is no report of this type of instant miracle, let alone a diabetic dying from one.

Getting sick is a process; getting well is also a process. Reiki helps in the process of healing by supporting the body's natural healing ability. Reiki can accelerate the healing process, but the effects of Reiki healing are generally accumulative, not instant. Reiki can help diabetics and they need not have any fear about receiving it.

A broken bone should not be treated with Reiki

Like the previous false belief this belief, was created on the false premise that Reiki instantly heals or can increase the healing process at warp speed. This false belief has several components. One, you do not channel Reiki to a person in an emergency with a broken bone until it has been placed back into the correct position and set. If Reiki is given at this time, it can begin to heal the bone and it will have to be re-broken and re-set at the doctor's office or hospital. Two, once the bone is set it will heal too quickly and can easily be broke again. Both are false.

If a person has broken a bone, Reiki will help to soothe the person and help with bleeding, if any, until help can be obtained to set the bone. As for healing too quickly and the bone being weak, that will never be a problem. When a bone heals it is usually stronger. Give Reiki to a person that has a broken bone as soon as you can and in all phases of the healing process.

Reiki Treatments should not be used with cancer

This false belief has prevented cancer clients from receiving Reiki for the fear it would speed up the cancer cells' division, which would cause the cancer and/or tumor to grow more quickly. This is absolute nonsense. That means Reiki would have to be selective by only going to the cancer cells to help them grow and multiply, therefore causing harm. Reiki will not cause harm. Reiki can help in all phases of cancer and treatment.

Reiki Treatments should not be used for venomous stings or bites

You should give Reiki to a person that has venomous stings or bites for as long as possible until medical treatment is available. Reiki will not speed up the effects of the poison. Instead it will help to keep the person calm and relaxed, and at the same time help with any swelling or pain. Of course, Reiki will also help with non-venomous stings or bites.

Life and death are one thread, the same line viewed from different sides.

- Lao Tzu

False Beliefs on Giving a Reiki Treatment

Intent is not needed during a Reiki Treatment

It is taught by some Reiki Masters and schools that you can give a Reiki Treatment without intent and focus, you do not have to do anything special when giving the treatment, or you can let your mind wander and even talk – the Reiki will go to where it's needed, eventually.

With the help of new books and teachings, this belief is rapidly being replaced with the understanding that you do need focus and intent during a Reiki Treatment for effective healing to occur. All major healing modalities understand this and use focus and intent in healing. Reiki is no different.

Focus is staying in the moment and concentrating on the task at hand, which would be giving the Reiki treatment. *Intent* is your state of mind in knowing Reiki's exact purpose for the treatment.

What I teach to accomplish focus and intent, so your mind does not wander, is to clear your mind as best you can of all thoughts. Then focus on the intent on what the Reiki Treatment is for and where it needs to be channeled. After a while you will become enmeshed in the feeling and flow of the Reiki and enter into what I call an "altered state." In this altered state your focus, intent and flow of Reiki become one. Speak only when necessary during the treatment.

Hands must touch the physical body during a Reiki Treatment

The key to this false belief is the word "must." Hands do not have to touch the physical body for Reiki to work. In fact, an increasing number of Reiki teachers and books being published do not recommend hand(s) touching the physical body during a Reiki Treatment.

Reiki will work with your hands on the body or above the body, but today it is wiser to work above the body for many reasons, such as an injury being too painful to touch, treatment needed is located in a private area, and you are working in the Aura. There are many more reasons why it's better to work above the body and I detail them in my books. Plus, in most U.S. states and cities (and eventually it may be all), unless you are a licensed clergyman, physiotherapist, massage therapist or medical doctor, the law prohibits the placing of hands on a client.

The following false belief will give more insight on this false belief.

Only one way to give a Reiki Treatment

Over the years Reiki teachers have facilitated classes and published books teaching a standard way to give a Reiki Treatment. The treatment consisted of a series of hand positions that were placed on the physcial body with a prescribed amount of time for each position, with the person lying on a massage table. Eventually during the treatment the hands just about touched the entire body and it took a long time to complete the treatment.

Now there are many new methods and techniques to give Reiki Treatments. These treatments are just as effective and cut the treatment time by half or more.

Treatments can also be given while the client is seated, standing or from long distance. What is evolving now with Reiki Treatments is that it is left to the Healer's intuitiveness on how to give a treatment, and each case may be different.

In my books, I give guidance regarding methods on how to perform Reiki Treatments for physical, mental, emotional, and spiritual issues, but I always leave it open if the Healer feels the need to alter the process I teach.

Fingers should be closed during a Reiki Treatment

The belief that fingers should be closed during a Reiki Treatment because it enables a stronger flow of Reiki and directs its flow more accurately is false. Fingers do not have to be closed when giving Reiki during a treatment.

Fingers can be spread open, half open or somewhere in between. The flow of Reiki will be the same no matter how you position your fingers. It's just a matter of preference for the Healer. As for the guidance of the Reiki, the intent of the treatment will help direct the flow of Reiki.

Only the right hand is used during a Reiki Treatment

This false belief originates from Reiki teachers overlapping Pranic and Chi healing systems with their Reiki teachings. These other two systems teach (although I have seen variations of this) projecting Chi or Prana through the right hand, while receiving Chi or Prana though the left.

A Reiki Healer can use one or both hands when channeling Reiki during a treatment. One hand is not stronger than the other, nor do you only receive Reiki with one hand and channel with the other. It's up to the Healer to decide what works best when giving a treatment. Also, it makes no difference whether you are "left" or "right" handed, or live in the northern or southern hemisphere – Reiki will flow the same out of one or both hands.

Fingers are placed in orifices during a Reiki Treatment

There are teachers, books and videos that proclaim the virtues of placing fingers in the mouth, ears, and nose for Reiki Treatments. The theory is the Reiki is channeled stronger with this method and it's easier to eliminate infections. Besides not being very hygienic and causing some people to shun a Reiki Treatment, this method is not needed. To treat these areas, hand(s) can be just 3 – 4 inches away from the body. I assure you the treatment will be just as effective without your digits in any orifice.

Feet and Crown Chakras should be avoided during a Reiki Treatment

"Feet should be avoided during a Reiki Treatment" arose from the false belief that all negative energy leaves the body via the feet; therefore, a Healer should avoid touching or standing below the feet. There is some truth to the belief about releasing negative energy (I call this negative energy "psychic debris"), but it can be from any place on the person, including the feet. Healers must protect[13] themselves from this psychic debris. If the Healer has performed protective measures before doing a Reiki Treatment, there is no need whatsoever to avoid any part of the body.

---

[13] There are many methods Healers can use to protect themselves from psychic debris. Sage, symbols, prayer, and white light are among them. I describe various methods in my books.

The false belief about the Crown Chakra arises from the misconception that the Healer might accidentally close it during a treatment, and this would cause problems or even death to the client. This false belief, although obscure and mostly spread in countries other than the United States, does keep surfacing. This belief will prevent people from receiving Reiki through one of the most important Chakras. This belief is false because you cannot open or close a Chakra accidentally or intentionally; although they may be blocked, the Healer cannot cause that.

If you would take, you must first give, this is the beginning of intelligence.

- Lao Tzu

**A good traveller has no fixed plans,
and is not intent on arriving.**

- Lao Tzu

False Beliefs on Reiki Healing

Reiki healing happens instantly

New Reiki Healers and people receiving a Reiki Treatment for the first time usually hold this false belief. It never ceases to amaze me when I receive an email from a person in this group stating they have taken my Healing Attunement one time or received a Reiki Treatment from another Healer one time and they were not healed instantly.

With any type of healing process, people have reasonable or unreasonable expectations. The people who have reasonable expectations understand getting sick was a process and getting well is also a process. People with unreasonable expectations want a quick fix. They are the people who contact me because they are disappointed that they weren't cured after only one treatment, even though they might have been sick for years. I don't imagine these same disappointed people would go to a medical doctor, receive a "treatment" of say a three-week course of antibiotics or other prescribed form of treatment, then call the doctor the next day and ask why they weren't healed in just one visit. Reiki will certainly help speed up the healing process, but the effects of Reiki healing accumulate over time, so more than one treatment is necessary.

It usually takes time to develop an illness, and when a person finally seeks treatment for it, it is understandable that quick results are desired. With any healing, you must have patience; you did not get into your situation over night. Healing is a process and will take time and effort depending on you and your circumstances. For example: if a person needs to heal physically by letting go of 20 years of anger, they might heal at a slower place than a person who needs to let go of only two years of anger. The reason being, 20 years of anger has taken more of a toll on the physical body.

As I mentioned before, if a person does not instantaneously exhibit any physical signs of healing after a Reiki Treatment, it does not mean that healing is not taking place. This only represents healing and changing is taking place in the Aura (emotional, mental, spiritual bodies) where the results cannot be seen until the healing resonates down to the physical body, which takes time. Of course, to what degree a person heals at each treatment depends on the individual circumstances at the time of the treatment and the strength of his or her immune system.

Reiki should be used as the sole method of treatment

Reiki should never be considered a sole method of treatment for any illness. If followed, this false belief can be fatal in some circumstances. Reiki should be used in conjunction with other healing modalities to help heal and change your life. A mention of other healing modality practitioners that could be sought in conjunction with Reiki might include medical doctors, allopaths, homoeopaths, naturopaths, chiropractors, ayurvedic physicians, acupuncturists, massage therapists, and/or hypnotherapists. The licensed health care professional you use depends on you and your situation. Remember, it is very helpful to use Reiki because it is your life force, which is needed in all healing modalities for them to be most effective.

As an example, if you have a headache from eating chocolate and use Reiki for it, the headache goes away. But the headache is from eating chocolate that you knew would give you a headache. You eat chocolate the next day and then the headache returns. You should consider another healing modality to help with the leading problem – the compulsion to eat chocolate. You might seek out a certified clinical hypnotherapist and use hypnotherapy to reprogram your subconscious mind to not crave or even desire chocolate.

If a Reiki Healer states that Reiki should be used as your only treatment and tells you other healing methods, including Western medicine should not be used, please do not follow that Healer's advice. The Healer's advice is a false belief and has the potential to cause harm.

Reiki can heal anything

If this false belief were true, Reiki healers would never die – they would just keep healing themselves. There isn't just one cure-all healing modality that can heal all illnesses. The belief should be "Reiki can help anything," then it would not be false.

Healing can be ambiguous. It can mean the removal of pain, and the underlying problem remains or it can be restoring complete balance after a cancer has been eradicated.

There are thousands of accounts about Reiki helping overcome every type of physical, mental, emotional or spiritual illness imaginable. I believe Reiki will help all illnesses, but it will not heal all illnesses. There is not a guarantee that a treatment will have the same level of results and timeline for healing with each person. The reasons for this I have mentioned several times before.

Always remember that healing is an everyday, ongoing process. You, and only you are responsible for doing all the groundwork (exercise, release work, diet, Reiki Treatments, medical treatment, etc.) to make healing possible.

He who talks more is sooner exhausted.

- Lao Tzu

False Beliefs on Reiki Distance Healing

Reiki 1ST Level Healers cannot send distance healing

Customarily, Reiki distance healing is taught to 2nd level healers during the Second Degree of Reiki training. The Reiki Symbols are introduced at that time, including the Long Distance Symbol. As a 2nd Level Reiki Healer you should be taught different techniques that use the symbols in sending distance healing. The techniques should include how to use your focus and intent to make the distance healing successful.

The reality is Reiki 1st Level Healers have the capacity to send distance healing by just using their intent for the healing to be received. They can send distance healing in an emergency or any other occasion in which healing is needed. The majority of the time, Reiki 1st Level Healers do not send distance healing because they are told they cannot, never told how and/or they progress to the 2nd Level Reiki teachings and Attunement before attempting distance healing as a 1st Level Healer.

Distance healing should not be sent without permission

You can send Reiki without permission to the past, present, and future. Sending distance healing should be thought of just like sending a prayer. You do not call the person to whom you want to send a prayer and ask if you can pray for them, you just go ahead send the prayer. Reiki distance healing is the same.

The challenge in asking permission for healing is there are many times when you want to help a person(s) who cannot be contacted. The person needing healing could be unconscious, (e.g., in a hospital, involved in a car wreck), traveling, lost, or otherwise unavailable. To receive permission before healing is sent with these conditions is difficult or near impossible. To deny people distance healing in these circumstances just does not make sense.

If you cannot let go of the false belief about sending Reiki without permission, here is what you do. Before you perform a distance healing, say a prayer that includes your intent for the Reiki and ask that the distance healing be received for the person's highest good.

Distance healings are not as strong as in-person healings

You can have the same great results from a Reiki distance healing treatment as an in-person treatment. Do not let any Healer tell you any different. If a Healer insists healing has to be performed in person, the likely motive for this is to get you into the office. Actually, a Healer who performs Reiki Treatments in person should be able to send distance healing. If they cannot, they are lacking in Reiki techniques and I would move on to another Healer.

Some people do prefer to receive a healing treatment in person because they enjoy the personal interaction with the Healer. This option is not available to all people for a few reasons. First, in-person treatments are usually a higher fee (although I have seen some fees for distance healing that are comparable) and could therefore be unaffordable. Or traveling is a problem; perhaps the Healer lives too far away, or a person's health will not permit them to travel. In these cases, distance healings are the only option.

Do not send distance healing to a person driving a car

This false belief is almost laughable if some Healers did not take it so seriously. The logic behind this belief is if you send Reiki distance healing when a person is driving a car, they will fall asleep at the wheel and crash. If this were true, any time you send Reiki distance healing the recipient would fall asleep, which does not happen. If you want to send Reiki to a person driving a car, do so. Reiki will not cause harm during any situation the person is in when receiving it.

**He who knows that enough is enough
will always have enough.**

\- Lao Tzu

**Knowing others is wisdom,
knowing yourself is enlightenment.**

- Lao Tzu

Reiki Symbol False Beliefs

There are only four Reiki Symbols

There are only four Reiki Symbols in Usui Reiki, but there are many variations of these four Reiki Symbols being used today. With all the variations of the four symbols, there is not one symbol that's more authentic or powerful than the other.

In this chapter you will be able to see illustrations of the different versions of the four symbols. Although the illustrations are not complete (Reiki Masters are always changing them), it will give you a very good idea of the diversity of the four symbols. If you are a Reiki Healer, you will most likely find your symbols represented in this chapter.

Not widely known is the fact that when Mikao Usui first started teaching Reiki there were no symbols in his system. He added the symbols to his teachings later on to help his students focus and direct their intent with Reiki healing. Also, in Japan, some Reiki Healers use an Attunement called a "Reiju" which does not include Reiki Symbols.

There is not a right or wrong set of symbols. What is wrong is when Reiki Healers claim their symbols are the only ones and/or the only symbols that can be used effectively. Use the symbols you have been attuned to, but understand they are not the only ones being used in Reiki. All symbols will work with the intent of the Healer.

I personally use and prefer the symbols that will be shown first in each set of illustrations. They're the symbols I have been attuned to and those that I teach and use to attune my students. I believe it's the set of four that is closest to the original symbols used by Usui, and I am sure some Reiki Masters would debate me on this.

This set of illustrations depicts the variations of the Reiki Power Symbol, which is also called the "Power Increase Symbol." Its name is Cho Ku Rei. The most common translation for the Power Symbol is "Put all the power in the universe here." The Power Symbol has many purposes when activated, but it is primarily used to increase the power (intent) of the Reiki or to focus Reiki on a specific location or for protection.

Symbol 1
Cho Ku Rei

Symbol 2
Cho Ku Rei

Reiki Power Symbol Illustrations

Symbol 3
Cho Ku Rei

Symbol 4
Cho Ku Rei

Symbol 5
Cho Ku Rei

Symbol 6
Cho Ku Rei

These illustrations show the variations of the Reiki Mental/Emotional Symbol, also called the "Emotional/ Mental Symbol," the "Mental Symbol" or the "Mental/ Emotional/Addiction Symbol." Its name is Sei He Ki. The most common translation for this is "God and humanity become One." This symbol has many uses, but is commonly used in emotional, mental, and addictive healing situations.

Symbol 7
Sei He Ki

Symbol 8
Sei He Ki

Reiki Mental/Emotional Symbol Illustrations

Symbol 9
Sei He Ki

Symbol 10
Sei He Ki

Symbol 11
Sei He Ki

Symbol 12
Sei He Ki

**Reiki Mental/Emotional Symbol Illustrations
continued on page 181**

Here are the diverse illustrations of the Reiki Long Distance symbol, also called the "Long Distance/Absentee Symbol." Its name is Hon Sha Ze Sho Nen. The name of this symbol has a few different interpretations. The one I use is "May the Buddha in me connect to the Buddha in you to promote harmony and peace." The symbol is very powerful and flexible and most Healers do not utilize its full capacity. When activated with specific intent, Reiki can be sent anywhere, anytime in the past, present, or future. Distance, time, and space are not a barrier when you use this symbol.

Symbol 13
Hon Sha Ze Sho Nen

Symbol 14
Hon Sha Ze Sho Nen

Reiki Long Distance Symbol Illustrations

Symbol 15
Hon Sha Ze Sho Nen

Symbol 16
Hon Sha Ze Sho Nen

Symbol 17
Hon Sha Ze Sho Nen

Symbol 18
Hon Sha Ze Sho Nen

Reiki Long Distance Symbol Illustrations
continued on page 185

These final illustrations reflect the differences of the Reiki Master Symbol named Dai Koo Myo. With this symbol, there are also several translations, but the one I use is "Great Being of the universe, shine on me, be my friend." The Master Symbol is known as the ultimate Reiki Symbol.

Symbol 19
Dai Koo Myo

Symbol 20
Dai Koo Myo

79

Reiki Master Symbol Illustrations

Symbol 21
Dai Koo Myo

Symbol 22
Dai Koo Myo

Symbol 23
Dai Koo Myo

Symbol 24
Dai Koo Myo

Reiki Master Symbol Illustrations
continued on page 189

Non-traditional symbols are stronger than traditional symbols

The four Reiki Symbols previously illustrated and all their variations are considered traditional Reiki Symbols. Any other symbols that are used in a Reiki System are considered non-traditional symbols.

The false belief that non-traditional symbols are stronger than traditional ones is told by Reiki Masters that have a vested interest in non-traditional Reiki Symbols being perceived as stronger. More on this later, but first let me tell you *how* such an abundance of Reiki non-traditional symbols have come into being.

Non-traditional symbols have been developed and created by different Reiki schools and Reiki Masters. They have intentionally changed the traditional Reiki Symbols, modified and/or adapted symbols from other healing systems or invented their own unique Reiki Symbols. Some even say new Reiki Symbols are channeled to them from spirits.

The new symbols are supposed to have unique powers or abilities from the traditional symbols and give you more options in healing and/or make you a stronger Healer. For example, one Reiki System uses 11 non-traditional symbols, and if you add the four traditional symbols, you have a mind boggling 15 symbols (some systems use even more). The truth is, you can have the same healing options with the four traditional symbols – it's all about your intent.

The purpose of the original four symbols was to give students a tool to focus their intent when working with Reiki. With the understanding that the student would use the symbols less and less as they became more proficient at using their intent. And eventually the time would arrive when the student would not need to use symbols at all.

The problem is some students mistakenly think the Reiki Symbols will do the work without using intent and using additional symbols will create even more results. However, once you learn how to use your intent efficiently, it isn't necessary to even use four symbols, let alone a myriad of symbols.

Now, back to why non-traditional symbols are created by Reiki Masters and schools and the vested interest they have in the symbols being perceived as stronger. The majority of them have created new symbols to make their Reiki unique, and by adding different symbols they can create additional Reiki Levels, degrees or new Reiki Systems, and this is okay. The problem is when they say their non-traditional symbols are stronger, new and improved, their energies are unique, etc. in order to fill their classes or market their Reiki Systems. Not only are the statements being made false, the statements create confusion with prospective Reiki Healers, generate ill will towards Reiki Healers using other Reiki Systems and give mixed messages to the public at large in regards to Reiki as a credible healing modality.

I understand some Healers like to use different symbols because they need all the extra ritual to focus their intent for different healing situations. However, to eventually progress in your healing abilities, you will have to rely on strong intent and not on symbols.

If you want to spend thousands of dollars for new Reiki Symbols and classes, you can do so, but it isn't necessary. I have found it best to keep it simple and that's why I use only four traditional symbols. The four symbols will work just as effectively with any intent you need to use with them.

The following are just a few samples of non-traditional Reiki Symbols being used today. I will give the symbol's name and the intent for the symbol, as I know it. Please be aware that the symbols I illustrate are examples to show my students and readers a variety of symbols being used today and not meant to be all-inclusive. As a matter of fact, other Healers might have different names and intent for the symbols I show and that is to be expected as nothing is carved in stone and the symbols can be very subjective from Healer to Healer. Plus, non-traditional symbols are being altered and invented constantly, so they are ever changing. If you do see a non-traditional symbol that you are using and I give a different name and/or intent, do not worry, your interpretation is correct for your usage.

If a Healer insists a non-traditional symbol has one absolute name and one absolute meaning, this can be true for the Reiki System they believe in. As I mentioned before, these symbols are ever changing and people in new and old Reiki Systems are giving non-traditional symbols new names and new ways to use them.

Please note most of the non-traditional symbols illustrated are mostly used in Attunements, although they can be used in treatments.

Symbol 25 Gnosa. This symbol's intent is to increase awareness of a connection with your source (God).

Symbol 26 Halu. The intent for this symbol is to stop subconscious undesirable life patterns and negative ego.

Symbol 27 Harth. This symbol's intent is to heal the emotional issues of the heart.

Symbol 28 Iava. This symbol's intent is to disperse untruths.

Symbol 29 Shanti or Shanty. The intent here is to heal the past by releasing fear, anger, and hurt.

Symbol 30 Zonar. The intent for this symbol is to release karma and expand consciousness.

Symbol 31 Templar. This symbol's intent is to manifest a Christ Consciousness.

Symbol 32 Motor Zanon. This symbol's intent is to help with the symptoms of the AIDS virus.

Non-traditional Symbol Illustrations

Symbol 25
Gnosa

Symbol 26
Halu

Symbol 27
Harth

Symbol 28
Iava

Non-traditional Symbol Illustrations

Symbol 29
Shanti or Shanty

Symbol 30
Zonar

Symbol 31
Templar

Symbol 32
Motor Zanon

Non-traditional Symbol Illustrations
continued on page 191

Reiki Symbols should be kept secret

Hawayo Takata originally taught that Reiki Symbols were to be kept secret until there is an energy exchange (which is usually money) and then the symbols can be revealed with instructions on how to use them to 2nd and Master Level Reiki students. It is told she even went to the extreme and had the symbols burned after classes to keep them a secret and swore the students to secrecy.

To further ensure the symbols secrecy a threat was started back in Takata's days that the symbols would lose their power for a person who viewed them before an Attunement. Or worse yet, the symbols would lose their power for the Healer who divulges them to a non-attuned Reiki person. This ludicrous threat really worked in the early days of Reiki in keeping the symbols secret and even to some extent today, but that is changing.

Today the necessity to keep Reiki Symbols secret is no longer important or of consequence for several reasons. One reason is the new generation of Reiki Healers, if asked, will share Reiki information with others and that includes the Reiki Symbols. They understand the old mentality of any and all Reiki teachings being kept secret has hurt the spread of Reiki and kept it from many people in need of it. Another reason is Reiki Symbols are impossible to keep secret because they are published in books (including mine) or on the Internet, available around the world to inform people seeking the truth about Reiki.

What's ironic about keeping the Reiki Symbols a secret is that they are not only used in Reiki[14]. They are used in different meditations and spiritual practices throughout the world, so they were never really so secret anyway.

Reiki Symbols must be drawn correctly for them to work

This is a common false belief I have to explain to my students frequently.

First of all, drawing the symbols in Reiki means tracing the symbols in the air with your fingers or eyes, or by visualizing yourself drawing them in your mind so you can activate[15] them with your intent. This is done when using Reiki Symbols during Reiki Attunements and Treatments. There are many ways to activate the symbols and it depends on what you were taught and which way works best for you.

Drawing the Reiki Symbols correctly and/or perfectly is not required for them to be activated. Nor does the method you use to draw the symbols make a difference in their effectiveness. The power of the Reiki Symbols does not come from drawing them perfectly. It comes from your intent to activate the symbols once you have been attuned to them. So, do not worry when you draw the symbols that they are not perfect; just draw them the best that you can and they will activate.

---

[14] That Reiki Symbols are only used in Reiki is a widely held misconception.
[15] When you activate a Reiki Symbol, it means you turn it on, make it work, go into action, etc.

Reiki Symbols have a power of their own

No matter what a Reiki Master tells you about Reiki Symbols having their own independent power, it is false. Unfortunately, it is not as simple as just drawing a Reiki Symbol and a power you need materializes. If this were true, the symbols would be magic[16] and Reiki is not magic. Each symbol does represent a specific meaning[17] for healing, but the symbols have no power of their own. You empower Reiki Symbols from your intent on how you will use them. They simply are tools to help focus your intent.

Non-healers cannot use Reiki Symbols

There is absolutely no harm in non-attuned people using Reiki Symbols. No person can tell another what to do or not do in regard to this. I understand old school Reiki Healers will insist that a non-healer cannot use the symbols, but how can they prevent it? And why would they want to if by some chance healing could occur by doing so?

In reality, most people will take Reiki classes or read books to receive directions on using the Reiki Symbols. With this being the case, Reiki Healers who are concerned about non-attuned people using Reiki Symbols can relax.

---

[16] See Chapter 16 for the false beliefs about Reiki being magic.
[17] The meaning for each symbol is very subjective in each Reiki system.

I have just three things to teach: simplicity, patience, compassion. These things are your greatest treasures.

- Lao Tzu

False Beliefs about Reiki Attunements

A Reiki Attunement is not a ritual

It is vehemently denied in some Reiki circles that a Reiki Attunement is a ritual. Apparently, they do not like the connotation of ritual; it sounds dark or too metaphysical.

They prefer to call a Reiki Attunement an initiation or spiritual ceremony. Nonetheless, a Reiki Attunement is a ritual performed by a Reiki Master – plain and simple.

Rituals have been used in all cultures throughout the history of man and are still used today. Some examples of rituals in our society are marriages, graduations, and baptisms.

Rituals are performed as gateways or passages for the human experience. They include ceremony and symbolism for the conscious and subconscious mind to remember and accept the importance of the ritual.

In a Reiki Ritual (Attunement) the Reiki Master uses symbols (symbolism) and uses the symbols and hand gestures (ceremony) in a prearranged way.

At times, I describe a Reiki Attunement as an initiation or spiritual ceremony, but I will define it to my students as a ritual.

All Reiki Attunements are performed the same way

All Reiki Attunements are not performed the same way. What is now called a Reiki Attunement might be one of a large (and growing) number of diverse Attunements. In fact, the number of versions of Reiki Attunements is impossible to determine with the many different Attunements being used today.

Here is a brief overview of the Usui Attunements, which are really the template and foundation for the majority of new Reiki Attunements that have been created.

In the classic Usui Reiki System[18], the Reiki 1st Level Attunement has four separate Attunements. It is common today to incorporate all four of those Attunements into one, which I do. The Reiki 2nd Level has only one Attunement, as does the Reiki Master Level. The major difference in the Usui Reiki Attunement method compared with other Reiki Attunement methods created is that the symbols are placed in the third eye, which I believe is a very significant, symbolic step.

During segments of the Usui Attunements, the Reiki Symbols are placed into the third eye and the hands. This is done while the hands are held over the head in a prayer position and the palms held opened in front of the Heart Chakra, respectively. In the Reiki 1st Level Attunement, only the Power Symbol is placed into the hands. During the Reiki 2nd Level Attunement, the Power, Long Distance and the Mental/Emotional Symbols are placed into the hands. During the Master Attunement, all four symbols are placed into the hands.

Next is just a sample of the different rituals that have been created in other Reiki Attunements.

➢ Nine Attunements (or more) for each level with different rituals for each Attunement
➢ Drawing large Reiki Symbols (sometimes as big as the student) on or around the body

---

[18] It's the system I teach in all my DVDs and books.

➤ Use different Chakras for each Attunement
➤ Place traditional and non-traditional symbols
  in different sequences into the Chakras
➤ Blowing air on a person in various places on the body
➤ Chanting and/or using mantras throughout
  the Attunement
➤ Different types of breathing systems used throughout
  the Attunement
➤ Reiki Master using different hands when placing
  symbols in and around the body
➤ Symbols placed into different areas around the body
➤ Students holding hands in different mudras[19] while
  receiving the symbols

These rituals can be done in different sequences or by adding different steps during the Attunement. There really is no end to what some Reiki Masters are doing with Attunements today.

As I mentioned with the symbols that exist now, there are no right or wrong symbols, there are no right or wrong Attunements. All the different Attunements will work if there is intent involved in the passing of the Attunement. I prefer and teach the classic Usui Reiki Level Attunements because the ritual is relatively simple, which makes it easy to pass Attunements. If you like a long Attunement process with plenty of ritual and are prepared to spend the extra money to learn how, there are plenty of options from which to choose.

---

[19] A mudra is a symbolic gesture made with the hand or fingers.

There are four Usui Reiki Level Attunements

In the classic Usui System of Reiki, there are only three Reiki levels, not four. The levels are 1st, 2nd and Master. There are three Reiki Attunements that correspond with each level.

Reiki Masters and schools created a 4th Reiki Level Attunement. The 4th is usually called the advanced level or Advanced Reiki Training (ART). The Attunement that corresponds with this level is given after the 2nd Level Attunement. This third Attunement, whatever they call it, only attunes a person to the Master Level and Master Symbol. The problem with this Attunement is that there are steps left out of it. One of the steps left out in this advanced Attunement is placing the Reiki Symbols in the Palm Chakras. The symbols need to be placed into the Palm Chakras to enable the person to perform Reiki Level Attunements on students, clients, relatives and friends.

It's my belief the reason this extra level has been created is simply so an additional Attunement/class is required and another set of fees can be charged. It also prevents the student (unless they pay for the final Master Level Attunement) from having classes and passing Attunements themselves (which could take students away from the Reiki Master). Usually the fee for the last Master Attunement is large, so some students are stuck on the advanced level even though they would like to continue to the Master Level. I use only the three Attunement process with the last Attunement passing all abilities to the Reiki Master Student. I don't believe in stringing the student along and withholding any of the Attunement process for additional fees.

The Hui Yin needs to be used in Reiki Attunements

Various Reiki Masters would like you to believe a muscular contraction of the Hui Yin point is a necessary part of giving Reiki Attunements. It is not. Of course, if you want to use it as part of the Attunement process, that's okay. As far as it being necessary, Attunements are being passed successfully around the world everyday without it being employed.

The Hui Yin point is between the anus and the genitals. It is claimed that tightening this point creates a higher frequency of energy when the energy (Reiki?) passes through it during the Attunement. You must hold (contract) the Hui Yin point the entire time you are giving the Attunement to prevent this special energy from escaping from this point. With some of the longer Attunements being used, this could mean holding (contracting) it for over half an hour or longer. If you are giving a series of Attunements, the process can become really tedious.

All healing practices are best with simple ritual and with strong intent and focus. If you feel you need the additional process of contracting the Hui Yin point, then by all means use it. Passing a Reiki Attunement without employing this process will work just as well.

The Violet Breath needs to be used in Attunements

The Violet Breath is a breathing technique used to place Reiki Symbol(s) into the Crown Chakra (or other Chakras) of the student during Attunements that may or may not incorporate the Hui Yin point. Just like in using the Hui Yin point, some Reiki Masters will insist this breath has to be used during Reiki Attunements to be passed successfully. Again, this is not true. Although using the Violet Breath can be used as an option, you can visualize, draw, and/or guide the symbols into the Chakras when needed during an Attunement. These methods will work just as well as the Violet Breath.

There are many versions of using the Violet Breath. Below is a sample of one way to give you an idea how it is used.

Step 1. Place your tongue on the roof of your mouth and at the same time contract the Hui Yin point.

Step 2. Inhale and visualize white or golden light flowing through your Crown Chakra, down the front of your body, then through the Hui Yin up your spine, until the light flows into in your head, filling it completely with the light.

Step 3. Imagine the light now in your head turning blue and beginning to rotate clockwise. While the blue light is rotating, imagine it turning to violet.

Step 4. Now, in this violet light visualize the symbol you will be using. Then breathe the Violet Breath (which includes the symbol) into the Chakra you want to place the symbol.

A lengthy waiting period is needed before receiving the next level Attunement

Years ago it was said you should wait at least one to two years after you received the Reiki 1st Level Attunement before taking the Reiki 2nd Level. Then you should wait three to ten years before taking the Master Attunement. Additionally, the three to ten years would give the student time to save for the $10,000.00 fee for the Master Level.

The world and the people in it are now evolving rapidly, so a lengthy waiting period between Attunements is no longer necessary. The old belief about the waiting period between the Attunements is now false. The 2nd Level can be taken immediately after the 1st Level. It is common for both the Reiki 1st and 2nd Level Attunements to be given during a weekend by Reiki Masters or received by my DVD Attunements. By taking the first two Reiki Levels back to back, you will be attuned to the three Reiki Symbols sooner, which will give more options for healing.

You should take the Master Attunement when you feel ready. It could be as little time as a few months or years. A Reiki 2nd Level Healer will know when they are ready for the Master Attunement.

Reiki Attunements should be kept secret

The Reiki Attunements need not be kept secret any more than the Reiki Symbols should be kept secret, as I explained in the previous Chapter. The myth behind this false belief is that if a person knows how the Attunement is performed, negative energy can be created and the Attunement will not be received and/or it won't be as strong. This is nonsense. Reiki cannot be a negative energy[20] and Attunements will always be received with the correct intent.

A person having or contemplating having a Reiki Attunement should be fully informed about the Attunement process. If the Reiki Master refuses to explain his or her Attunement ritual, I would move on to another Reiki Master who will not keep it a secret from you. Of course, some people do not care about the process or how it works, just that it does.

The metaphor I use for this is, say you would like and/or need a medical procedure. You want to obtain more information about the process before you experience it, but the doctor does not want to tell you anything about it. He just wants you to pay and have it done. I would hope in a case like this you would find a doctor who would be open with you. It's the same with Reiki Masters – if they are not forthcoming with answers, find one who will be.

Reiki Long Distance Attunements do not work

This false belief most likely will be one of the most controversial in this book because of all the hypocrisy and money issues linked to it. I say hypocrisy because Healers who say this belief is true will turn around and teach long distance healing and state it will work. The only problem with this is long distance healing uses the same concept as long distance Attunements.

---

[20] See Chapter 13, Reiki False Belief: Reiki is a dual energy.

The Healers who support this belief being true usually cite views expressed by other Masters (like themselves) who have a vested interest (charging fees) in passing Attunements in person; therefore, the belief is also linked to money issues. What's sad is most of the Masters who use this belief know it is false. Some try to get around the bad karma of using the false belief by stating that long distance Attunements do work, but not very well and should only be used in emergencies.

I would love for one or a group of these Healers who deny the success of long distance Attunements to address the tens of thousands of Healers around the world (maybe in a stadium) who have received Attunements via DVDs, video, Internet, etc., and who have healed themselves and others and are doing great healing work. What would or could they say to this huge audience? "Non-Healers, you all are lying or mistaken about your healing. Even if you have healed yourself or others, it's not the correct way. But there's hope for you. Take my class and Reiki Attunements and your healing will be correct."

The bottom line is Attunements work just as well in person as from a distance and most of the Reiki Masters who deny this know it is true. If they do not, they are lacking in Reiki teachings and I will take the opportunity now to enlighten them.

First of all, Reiki Attunements are done on an energetic level rather than a physical one. All Reiki Masters have to agree on this. The only physical touching that can be done is tapping of the hands, touching the shoulders, and blowing air, which is really optional. All that is needed for a Reiki

Long Distance Attunement to be passed successfully is the ritual (Attunement) that includes the Reiki Master's intent (belief) to give a Reiki Attunement and the recipient's intent (belief) to receive the Attunement.

Now these Healers (the ones who state long distance Attunements do not work) might say I have a vested interest in my Reiki DVD Attunements, and of course I do, but there are some big differences with what I believe. I feel a person should receive a Reiki Attunement any way they prefer and/or can afford. All options to receive Attunements will work and my DVD Attunement programs are one of the options. And I am interested in as many people as possible in whatever way they choose being able to have Reiki Attunements.

Here are a few excerpts from my first book about my firsthand experiences with this false belief:

The Reiki Masters who wrote to me always stated the same thing, "You can only perform the Attunement in person." My reply was always that maybe *they* cannot pass an Attunement using a video as a medium, but I certainly can and do, along with other Reiki Masters that have the knowledge and ability. Then I would inquire about the people who have taken the Attunements and claim they have received them. What about their statements acknowledging they now channel Reiki to themselves and others? Are these people mistaken or making it up?

I always knew these people received the Attunement, and they knew they received it, so as a third party these Reiki Masters were passing judgment. In all spiritual paths, including Reiki, you are taught not to judge. Usually, I wouldn't receive a response after my reply. A few that did answer would acknowledge that maybe there is some truth in what I said and maybe there was room in the world for different Reiki beliefs. They also should have realized that my programs were not produced for everybody, just the students that were drawn to me.

This is a big world and there is plenty of room and a great need for all Reiki Healers regardless of their beliefs and teachings. All Reiki Healers and Masters should focus on the healing at hand (no pun intended) and not be judgmental of anything, least of all Reiki.

Free Reiki Attunements are free

First of all, there is nothing for free in this world, and that includes Reiki Attunements. Eventually there is always an exchange for anything that is received, on some level (physical, mental, emotional or spiritual). For every action there is a reaction. If you accept a Free Reiki Attunement without a conscious payment (whatever that is – money, babysitting, a barter, etc.), the payment for it will happen at some time in the future in some form, and you will have no control over its content. It is best to pay consciously, even if it is a small donation for any Attunement.

Regrettably, a few Reiki Masters devised a gimmick to increase their practice (business) by giving a "free" Reiki 1st Level Attunement that they state will only last a limited time. After the limited time period for this free Attunement has expired and if the person wants the Attunement to last, the person will be charged a fee and will be required to pay for a Reiki class.

The main problem with this is that it is impossible to *make* a Reiki 1st Level Attunement last for a limited period of time. Once you receive a 1st Level Reiki Attunement it will last your whole life. Another problem is, you don't know what you are getting with a free gimmick Attunement. What type of intent and Attunement is being passed? I would steer clear of a Master who makes this or a similar offer.

A Reiki Attunement is needed to become a Healer

You do not need a Reiki Attunement to become a Healer. Do not let anyone tell you any different. As I mentioned before, every person is a natural Healer. The advantage of using Reiki is that it shows you a process (ritual) with tools (symbols) that give you direction and guidelines on using your natural healing ability, which most people need.

Reiki Masters who are so adamant about a person needing Reiki Attunements to become a Healer are being judgmental and usually have a hidden agenda (consciously or unconsciously) for students to learn Reiki from them. What is ironic is some of these Healers that state you cannot become a Healer without Reiki Attunements have modified or invented new processes they call Reiki. If you have a healing process that will guide your healing ability, use it. You do not need Reiki. It's all about the end results (healing), not which method that you prefer to accomplish this.

A special power is transferred during a Reiki Level Attunement

To build up their mysticism, ego, or power, Reiki Masters (not all, of course) might like you to believe that a special power transfers[21] between a Reiki Master and a student during a Reiki Level Attunement. This is not true.

What does happen is that through the Reiki Attunement, the Master empowers the student(s) to be able to use Reiki, but does not give them a special power. This empowerment is done with ceremony and symbolism, in other words, ritual. There is an actual clearing of the Chakras by the Master during the Reiki Attunement so that Reiki will flow smoother for the student.

You should not repeat the same Reiki Attunement

Even though Reiki Level Attunements last for life, repeating Reiki Attunements can be beneficial, especially if you haven't been using Reiki for a while. By receiving Reiki Attunements again (re-attuning), you can help clear any blockages or psychic debris that has accumulated since you last received the Attunement. Of course, what level Attunement you decide to take over all depends on what level you feel you need, as well as what Reiki Levels you have completed.

---

[21] There are so many outlandish stories about what happens during an Attunement that the list would be many pages. One example (besides the special power being transferred) is that during the Attunement the Master transfers a special program (like a download) to the inner being of the student so they can use Reiki.

I have been told that in Japan, a student receives an Attunement from his teacher every time they meet. I do not know the validity of this, but it makes good sense. You will know when you need to be re-attuned. Go ahead and repeat an Attunement as you become aware of the need for it.

The eyes need to be closed when receiving a Reiki Attunement

Eyes do not need to be closed when receiving a Reiki Attunement. This belief is proven false everyday by the students who take my open eye Reiki DVD Attunements. Your eyes can be open or closed during a Reiki Attunement. Either way, the Attunement will be passed.

The false belief that the student's eyes must be closed during an Attunement ties into the mentality that Reiki needs to be kept secret, which is threaded into the many false beliefs in this book. Again, whether eyes are open or closed during a Reiki Attunement should all depend on the preference of the person receiving the Attunement.

Intent is not needed when giving a Reiki Attunement

Just like intent is important when using Reiki Symbols, intent is required and is the most important aspect in giving a Reiki Attunement. In Reiki Attunements, you must make your intent clear on which Attunement you are going to give before you perform it. For example, if you are going to give a Reiki 1st Level Attunement, you must make your intent clear that it is a Reiki 1st Level Attunement.

I recommend saying the type of Attunement in a prayer or state it silently to yourself at the beginning of any Attunement you are going to give. The Reiki Attunement will then be passed on to the student(s) during the process.

A new Reiki Attunement cancels previous Attunements

It is not possible to lose or cancel a previous Reiki Attunement. The reason this false belief comes into play is students sometimes want to receive different Attunements so they can be attuned to different symbols. There are concerns that the ability to use the other symbols from the previous Attunements will be lost. This will not happen.

Also, a Reiki Master might tell a student that the Attunement they received was not correct (for whatever reason) and insist they receive new Attunements in order to cancel the previous ones. All subsequent Attunements you receive from another Master will help clear and reinforce your Chakras, but will not cancel the previous Attunements. All Reiki Attunements last for life.

One can not reflect in streaming water. Only those who know internal peace can give it to others.

- Lao Tzu

He who does not trust enough, will not be trusted.

- Lao Tzu

False Beliefs about the Reiki Healer

ELEVEN

Reiki Healers do not get sick

It would be great it this false belief were true, but Reiki Healers do get sick, they age and eventually leave their physical bodies like everyone else. This belief is sometimes used as an incentive to have a person become a Reiki

Healer. The good news is if the person decides to become a Reiki Healer and use Reiki regularly and maintain a balance on all levels (physically, mentally, emotionally and spiritually), they will not get sick as often. When they do happen to get sick, it is not as severe.

All Reiki Healers have the same healing ability

In every line of work, sports, creative endeavors, etc., there are a few people who have a higher ability and Reiki is no exception. For example, one medical doctor will say a medical procedure is impossible because of his/her skills, ability, and teachings, while another doctor will say it can be done because of his/her ability, skills, and teachings, and they prove it by performing the procedure successfully.

All Reiki Masters and Healers do not have the same healing ability. The reason for this is not because of a system of Reiki or Reiki Symbols. They have a higher level of healing ability for many reasons, including natural abilities, stronger intent, balance in all their bodies (mental, physical, spiritual, emotional), and additional experience in improved Reiki techniques. All of these are within the Healer's power to work on improving Reiki healing ability, except the natural ability.

A Reiki Healer can make up for any lack of natural ability by having strong intent when channeling Reiki, keeping balanced and clear on all bodies, and practicing and learning new healing techniques. However, having said all that, any Healer can have days when his or her Reiki is not quite as strong, and the reasons are not always known.

When this happens, I recommend taking a week off from Reiki and when you resume healing with Reiki, you will be back to normal.

A Reiki Healer needs to have hot hands

Many Reiki Healers become concerned that their healing ability has diminished if heat is not felt in their hands during a treatment. Healers' hands do not always become hot during a treatment and it is not a requirement for a successful Reiki Treatment. Hands can become cool or warm, vibrate, tingle or a combination of different feelings during a treatment. No matter what sensations of the hands the Healer feels or notices during a Reiki Treatment, the Reiki is flowing. It is interesting to note that during each Reiki Treatment the hands can have different sensations, depending on the circumstances of the person receiving the treatment.

A Reiki Healer lives a
shorter physical life

This false belief comes from the assumption a Reiki Healer is using his or her own personal life force. This false belief is coupled with the belief that a person only has so much Reiki to use in any given physical lifetime, so a Reiki Healer is expending personal life force in healing others, which, in turn, shortens the life span. Both are completely false. Although the Healer does have his or her own life force (Reiki) within, when channeling Reiki to others, it comes from outside the physical body, from the source of Reiki. There is an infinite supply of Reiki to channel when needed.

People with their own personal agenda (which includes the fear of Reiki shortening lives) to keep people (relatives, friends, etc.) from becoming Reiki Healers are usually the ones who spread this false belief.

A Reiki Healer cannot take on the symptoms of the client

This belief is false, as any Healer that has been unlucky enough to experience the symptoms of their clients will tell you. This transference of symptoms of the client to the Healer can manifest in many ways. It can be the same actual pain in the same area in the body as in the client's. If it's emotional or mental distress the client is having, the Healer may experience the same emotions and feelings. Or the Healer might feel drained physically, emotionally and mentally after the treatment.

To prevent this transference of symptoms a Healer must protect[22] him/herself during a Reiki Treatment or Attunement. If the Healer is not protected, besides the unpleasant experience of the client's symptoms, there can be an eventual buildup of psychic debris in the Healer's Aura. This buildup might not pose a problem in the short term, but it can in the long run. Better to be safe and protect yourself.

You do not have to practice Reiki

As part of their sales pitch, many Reiki schools proclaim that once you become a Reiki Healer you do not have to

---

[22] It's up to the Healer on which of the many methods to use. I give suggestions in my books.

practice. Common sense should tell you this is false. Like anything else you want to excel in or stay at the same level, you need to practice. It's the same with Reiki. You need to practice to maintain your healing skills.

A person needs to be a Buddhist to become a Reiki Healer

It is assumed by people who are uninformed about Reiki that you need to be a Buddhist or begin practicing Buddhism to become a Reiki Healer. Although it is thought in some Reiki circles (I believe this myself) that the original Reiki System was based on Buddhist Sutra and Tantra, you do not have to be a Buddhist or believe in Buddhism to be a Reiki Healer. Individual Reiki Masters may reflect their different religious influences in their Reiki teachings. It would be a good guess this is how this false belief started.

A Reiki Healer must be vegetarian

This is another common false belief. There is no direct connection between stronger Reiki healing and being a vegetarian. There are great Reiki Healers who are not vegetarians, and some even smoke and drink. The diet is a matter for each individual to choose. Of course, if a person feels his or her Reiki will benefit by being a Vegetarian, it will.

Reiki Masters may outline a specific diet before Reiki Attunements or Treatments. How much of the diet the person should follow is still up to the individual. If a Reiki Master insists you follow the diet or the Reiki Attunement or Treatment will not work, get yourself another Master, one who will not force individual beliefs about diets on you by using the threat that Reiki will not work. There are many Masters who will suggest a diet and ask you to follow it as best you can.

Reiki Healers can lose their healing ability

I receive inquiries from Reiki Healers concerned that Reiki stopped flowing while they were channeling it, that they have lost their healing ability. If a person has been attuned to Reiki, I guarantee Reiki is still flowing. Just because you don't physically feel Reiki does not mean it has stopped flowing. At different times Reiki might flow with different intensities in a treatment or Attunement, but that level of intensity is what is needed at that moment for the person receiving it.

People are accustomed to a physical confirmation to prove something is working, but there are times with Reiki where there are very minimal, if any, signs. Each Reiki session and Reiki Attunement stands on its own and is a unique experience. Once you are attuned to Reiki it is for life and it will always flow.

If a Healer is still concerned that Reiki has stopped flowing, even though one cannot lose the ability to heal, I recommend re-attuning to the last Reiki Level received for clearing and reinforcement, then taking a week off. It will remedy the perceived situation.

A Reiki Healer should be healed before giving Reiki to others

Due to the fact that every Reiki Healer is a healing work-in-progress, if this belief was valid, then there would be very few Reiki Healers available.

If you are a Reiki Healer, you do not have to be healed completely before you help others with Reiki. Most Reiki Healers start out with Reiki to help themselves, then it progresses to healing others. It is a personal choice when a Reiki Healer decides to help others, but it is not necessary for a Healer to be completely healed before that happens. As a matter of fact, as a Reiki Healer is healing others, the process is usually helping to heal the Healer also.

One who is too hesitant on his own views, finds few to agree with him.

- Lao Tzu

False Beliefs about Reiki Masters

TWELVE

$10,000 is the fee to become an authentic Reiki Master

When Reiki was first taught in the West, it was common for a $10,000 fee to be charged for the Reiki Master Level. Hawayo Takata started this fee with the explanation that a high fee was part[23] of the Usui System because it represented value and commitment on the part of the person who wished to become a Reiki Master. I still remember my first Reiki Master telling students about this fee and being shocked when I realized that most people could never become a Master Healer given those financial requirements.

The Master fees started to come down in the mid-eighties when Iris Ishikura, a Reiki Master who received the Master Attunement and training from Takata, went against Takata's policy and started charging lower fees. Since this time, fees have slowly continued to come down where now a Reiki Master Attunement and training is affordable. Never again will a person need to pay a $10,000 fee to become a Reiki Master.

Unbelievable as it may seem, there are still a few select schools that will charge a $10,000 fee. Besides charging the high fee, they also require the students to complete an apprenticeship for a period of at least one year under the same Reiki Master who trained them. In addition, once the new Master begins to teach, it is only under the bestowing Master's supervision for one year, and this Master receives all of the course fees. The new Master may not pass a Master Level Attunement for three years to ensure fees are not taken from his/her Master.

In reality, with all of these conditions, the person is paying over $20,000 (depending on the value you place on working for a year and the fees generated from classes.)

---

[23] It has since been discovered a high fee was not required by Usui to become a Reiki Master.

Then, to add insult to injury, you cannot teach other Masters for three years which will slow down the ability to recoup training fees. The business model these schools use for Reiki training is truly unfair, and some might say unscrupulous.

Reiki Masters are Spiritual Masters

The term "Master" as used in Reiki Master does not have the same meaning (as some would like you to believe), as a spiritual master who is an enlightened being or is self-realized, which can take a lifetime of work. "Master" in Reiki Master is meant to express mastery of the Reiki healing process and technique. Now, this does not mean a Reiki Master cannot be an enlightened being, and I am sure there might be a few in the world today who are. I do believe a true Reiki Spiritual Master would not proclaim they are one to the world because they would find it unnecessary to do so and maybe that's why they are hard to find. For that reason, the Reiki Master that claims he or she is a Reiki Spiritual Master is suspect, in my opinion.

Reiki Grand Masters are special

The title of *Reiki Grand Master* is surfacing more and more and the cause seems to be ego driven. Do not let this title intimidate or give you the impression that this person is special. I would think if anybody should have the title Reiki Grand Master it would be Usui, who is the founder of modern-day Reiki.

A Reiki group[24] first used the title Reiki Grand Master for the leader of its organization. Since then some Reiki Masters who teach students to be teachers started calling themselves Reiki Grand Masters. And even Reiki Masters that do not teach Reiki have jumped on the bandwagon and added Grand to their title for extra prestige.

All Reiki Masters are equal in that they all have the ability to pass Attunements and Reiki teachings on to others, that is, unless they are unfortunate to have had only the advanced level[25] Reiki Master Attunements. If you come across a Reiki Master who has added "Grand" to his/her title, I would suggest you ask why, then see how the response resonates with you before you select them for any Reiki needs.

Independent Reiki Masters are not true Reiki Masters

The term "Independent Reiki Master" was first used years ago to refer to Reiki Masters who preferred to go their own way and did not join a few collective groups of Reiki Healers at that time. The term "Independent Reiki Master" coined by these groups was meant to be a negative term, to insinuate that the Reiki practiced by these Independent Reiki Masters was somehow defective or phony. In other words, these Independent Masters did not charge high fees, did not keep secrets, used different Reiki Symbols and teachings, and wanted to spread Reiki to as many people as possible, not just to the ones who could afford it. Today, the majority of Reiki Masters are Independent.

---

[24] Reiki Alliance
[25] This is explained in Chapter 10: There are only four Usui Reiki Level Attunements.

Reiki Masters are responsible for miracles

This false belief relates to the false belief that Reiki can heal all illnesses[26].

A conscientious Reiki Master knows that he or she is not a miracle worker, that they merely channel Reiki and are not responsible for the outcome once it is received. A miraculous, instantaneous healing event can occur, but most of the time, healing is a timeline process. If a Reiki Healer touts him/herself as a miracle worker, quickly move on to another Reiki Healer. If clients tout the healings that they have received from a particular Healer, I would certainly look into using that Healer.

It takes years to become
a Reiki Master

As I mentioned before, years ago it was said you should wait at least one to two years after you received the Reiki 1st Level Attunement before taking the Reiki 2nd Level. Then you wait three to ten years before you take the Master Attunement. A person really had to adhere to the above policy because there was no other way to become a Reiki Master at that time.

It does not take years to become a Reiki Master anymore. With different options available for Reiki training, people are becoming Reiki Masters based on their own timelines and needs. This new paradigm for the changing world really upsets Reiki Masters in certain circles, especially the ones who have been Masters for years and their classes

---
[26] False belief in Chapter 7: Reiki can heal anything.

and fees are based on long-term training. There is nothing wrong with how these Masters teach, and some people prefer to go that route. For the people that want to become Reiki Masters at their own pace, the knowledge and guidance is available in books, DVDs, on the Internet and through correspondence courses.

All Reiki Masters are teachers

Not all Reiki Masters are teachers. This is a false belief usually held by people who are unfamiliar with Reiki. A Reiki Master can just give healing treatments or teach and give Reiki Level Attunements. A Reiki Master can also teach other Reiki Masters how to teach others.

The problem arises again as a Reiki Master may only have received the advanced Attunement[27]. If this is the case, this Master is lacking the Attunement that will enable him or her to pass and teach Attunements. This means a limitation to only giving Reiki Treatments. I have heard from some Masters who are in this situation and are completely unaware of the limitations they have. So, it always behooves you to quiz a Reiki Master on his or her personal training and capabilities.

Reiki Masters cannot give Attunements without Reiki Symbols

If a Reiki Master has reached a level where Reiki Symbols are no longer needed as tools, it is certainly possible to give an Attunement without symbols. The Reiki Master

---

[27] This is explained in Chapter 10: There are only four Usui Reiki Level Attunements.

would just use intent throughout the Attunement for what needs to happen. Granted, very few Reiki Masters ever reach this level and even if they do, many prefer the familiarity of the Reiki ritual. As I stated before, when Reiki was first re-discovered the Reiki Symbols were not used in Attunements, so it should not be a surprise that it can be possible to pass Attunements without the symbols.

To realize that you do not understand is a virtue; Not to realize that you do not understand is a defect.

- Lao Tzu

Common Reiki
False Beliefs

It's easy to start a Reiki business

A few Reiki schools that teach traditional and non-traditional Reiki have made it appear easy to start a Reiki business and make a substantial income. Even Internet sites are popping up left and right promising business secrets that show a way for Reiki Healers to make six figure incomes every year with their step-by-step Reiki business programs.

If you pay a large fee for Reiki training because you think you will make a large income (as some Reiki schools and the Internet ads lead you to believe), you are going to be sorely disappointed. The truth is, Reiki schools and the Internet sites selling this concept are the only ones who will make the large income from the fees you pay them to train you.

Before I get into exposing the nuts and bolts of the false claims of a fortune to be made in starting a Reiki business, let me first explain about going into Reiki as a business. The realistic concept with Reiki is that people become Healers not to make money, but to help themselves, relatives and friends. Then a few out of this group will start working part-time with clients charging fees. Occasionally, a few of these "part-time" Healers begin a full-time business teaching Reiki and seeing clients. The majority of Reiki Healers who have a successful part-time or full-time Reiki business are people who started out to help themselves, relatives, and friends, and it progressed from there. They never attended any type of Reiki training that promised a large income - the large income just happened naturally.

Another factor that usually prevents people from starting their own Reiki business (which these schools and websites fail to tell you) is that it's getting harder and harder to obtain a business license to practice Reiki in most states and major cities unless you already have a license for another type of healing modality[28]. The primary reason for this is the "hands on" techniques[29] taught by Reiki schools and used by some Reiki Healers. It is the "hands on the body" techniques that concern licensing authorities (i.e., state and city governments) requiring some measure of regulation. Eventually, I think a majority, if not all, of these governing authorities will enact laws, ordinances, or other regulations regarding "hands on" techniques before a license will be issued.

First, let's talk about the websites with the super business secrets for sale. Usually, the site will use a person who claims to be a Reiki Master, who gives classes and seminars around the world, and makes a six-figure-plus income. The pitch will be something about you following their step-by-step instructions (for a fee, of course) and becoming as successful as they are. What these people are saying about themselves may be true (although I have my doubts). The stark reality is that their plan will not work for 99.99 percent of the people and the reason for that is quite simple. They are not concerned about healing, just about making money. Very few people are dynamic public speakers or superstar salespersons, so they will not be able to mirror what these "pitch men or women" claimed to have done. Even if a small portion of the people were able to be successful implementing these plans, cities would be saturated with Reiki seminars and classes, attendance would be down, and no one would be earning a six-figure income.

---

[28] Nurses, hypnotherapists, massage therapists, chiropractors, etc.

[29] Many Reiki Masters teach hands-off-the-body healing techniques, including myself.

The Reiki schools that promise a large income from a Reiki business are set up as multi-level marketing programs, or you might even say a variation of a pyramid[30] plan. This sort of program involves the Reiki School charging a high fee to the new student to learn Reiki. Then they encourage the student to charge high fees to train new Reiki Healers. The catch is to charge the high fees to other students who must train with a teacher authorized from the school in a required number of classes for which the student is then made responsible for recruiting new students. This could take a year or longer depending on how successful the new Healer is in finding students for the classes. The bad news is all the fees for these classes go to a teacher authorized by the school, not the new Reiki Healer.

To fill the required classes the new Healer usually recruits all his or her friends and relatives, typically exhausting all student resources before acquiring the requisite number of classes needed to be certified to teach. The schools are aware that most of the Healers will never make the class requirement and they do not care. They have already benefited from the initial high fee charged to the student and any classes the new Reiki Healer does sponsor is found money.

Now, if a Reiki student makes it through this process and sponsors enough classes, he or she will be certified by the school to be able to reap the rewards by doing the same program to future (unsuspecting) Reiki students. The Reiki school's "cut of the action" does not end there. The Reiki

---

[30] A financial scheme where the first people putting in money (people at the top of the pyramid) make the money. The last people putting in the money (at the bottom of the pyramid) lose their money.

student (who is now officially a Reiki teacher) must give a percentage back to the school for all classes taught, pay an annual fee to be certified, and buy all Reiki materials from the school. The reason these schools say they have programs like this is "to keep the continuity and integrity of Reiki intact." I say the main reason is money.

The reality is that students get lured into paying a high fee to learn Reiki based on a false incentive of someday having their own lucrative Reiki business, which never materializes. And the schools continue to make the six figure incomes.

Children should not receive or be taught Reiki

This false belief is generated from the premise that Reiki is too strong of a force and will harm children, that their systems cannot handle it, which is false. Again Reiki can never harm you, and this includes children. Babies and young children can and should receive Reiki. They are, however, much more sensitive to Reiki and do not require as much as an adult. Channeling Reiki to small children and babies is best done when holding them or while they are sleeping. With older children it is appropriate to use the same techniques as with adults.

The true source of Reiki is within us

The source of Reiki is not within us even though we do have Reiki throughout our physical bodies. Reiki is the universal life force and it comes from a source outside us.

This source can be called anything you choose to call it - a higher power, a higher dimension, God, etc. Not one person in the physical world can completely understand, explain and verify the exact details and nature of this source, although many have different beliefs and theories.

Clairvoyants have stated that Reiki comes down from above, then enters the top of the head (Crown Chakra) and flows through the body and out the hands. I personally believe it flows into all of our Chakras, including the feet, but with the preponderance flowing through our Crown Chakra, which is most likely what the clairvoyants see.

Reiki automatically protects you from harm

Reiki does not automatically protect you from harm. It's not that simple, as some Healers will lead you to believe. You must actively use your intent and different methods daily to protect yourself. Most Healers know of the options for protection methods and use their own personal choices.

Besides protecting yourself from the day-to-day hazards of life, you must also protect yourself and others before, during, and after Reiki Treatments and Attunements. Psychic Debris that is released during this time can become attached to you and/or stay in the room to become attached to someone else, or even a pet. Healers often refer to this as "picking up things from their clients." This release is common, but with the correct safeguards in place there is no need to worry. Simply understand that just because you are attuned to Reiki, it will not automatically protect you from harm, and there are measures that you can and should take to protect yourself.

Reiki is not channeling

When giving Reiki in a treatment you are indeed channeling Reiki. "Channeling Reiki" and "giving Reiki" are one and the same.

The confusion of the term "channeling" can be linked to what a medium does when they connect to the spirit world and receive information. That is also called channeling.

Once Healers receive a Reiki Attunement, they can be referred to as Reiki Channels, which means they have an ability to send Reiki through their own bodies to themselves and others. It does not mean that they can talk to spirits from the "other side," although some Reiki Healers can.

Reiki can only be used for physical conditions

This false belief is widespread with people who only have a limited knowledge of Reiki and what it can do. Surprisingly, it is also held by Reiki Healers who have only been taught techniques using Reiki with the physical body.

Reiki can be used to assist in all mental, emotional and spiritual issues, and the best way involves techniques using the Aura. If you are a Reiki Healer who is only trained in techniques for the physical body, it would behoove you to learn specific healing methods[31] for mental, emotional

---

[31] "*Reiki the Ultimate Guide,* Vol. 3: Learn New Reiki Aura Attunements, Heal Mental & Emotional Issues," will give you options for healing mental, emotional and spiritual issues.

and spiritual issues. If you are seeking Reiki Treatments for such, make sure your Healer has training for it.

Reiki is a dual energy

Reiki is not a dual energy. A dualistic form of energy can be used in a good way or a harmful way. Electricity is an example of a dual energy. It can be used for good or it can be deadly.

Apparently, this false belief was started as a threat that Reiki was going to be used for harm by some unethical Healers who wanted control of a situation or person. Remember, Reiki can never cause harm, which means it can never be used for harm.

Physical contact is needed for Reiki to start flowing

To make Reiki flow, all you have to do is have the intention to make it flow, and it will. Your hands do not have to touch a person's physical body. The belief that you must actually touch the physical body for Reiki to flow is linked to older Reiki teachings that, unfortunately, still exist.

Reiki with a Trademark is more effective

The limited number of people and schools that have trademarked the Reiki Systems they have invented would like people to believe that Reiki with a trademark is more effective. As I explained in Chapter 10, one Reiki System is not more effective than another. The basic teachings of Reiki cannot be trademarked like the basic teachings of religions leaders, such as Buddha or Jesus. I feel that trying to trademark the universal life force will lead to bad karma and that doing so is tied to ego, control, and perhaps greed. I understand a few have been successful with this by working the trademark system, but they really have not trademarked Reiki, just a name they have attached to Reiki.

Even more disturbing, a few Healers with trademarks have been involved in lawsuits throughout the years fighting over the names of their Reiki Systems. My contention is Reiki should be about the healing and not about lawsuits of Reiki names and trademarks. This type of negative activity, in my opinion, acts against the basic ideology behind using Reiki for healing and the promotion of positive emotions and growth.

Reiki is magic

Of course Reiki is not magic. Religious groups who do not want Reiki used by its members spread this belief. Their religious doctrines usually are in opposition to magic, so they classify Reiki as magic. I find it ironic that these doctrines usually have hands-on healing practices and these are not magic. Another reason Reiki might be called magic by people is because it works so well at times, and people who are not aware of why and how Reiki works have no other explanation.

Reiki is a cult

The early Reiki origins and how it was taught in the West are responsible for this false belief. The secrecy of Reiki teachings and the control used by Reiki Masters over their students gave the appearance of Reiki being a cult. People looking at Reiki from the outside could not help but come to that conclusion. This false belief has kept many people from pursuing Reiki. Luckily, with all the Reiki information available today and the openness of the new generation of Reiki Healers, this false belief is fading from the rumor mill.

Spirit possession can manifest when using Reiki

I do believe that problems could arise if a Reiki Healer or any other person conducts a séance or actively tries to contact spirits/entities without proper knowledge[32] and protection is not in place when doing so. However, demons or spirits with ill intent will not possess a Reiki Healer, client and/or student during a Reiki Treatment or Attunement. Reiki is always for the highest good, and demons or spirits with ill intent do not fit into that category.

Reiki works on cars, computers, appliances, etc.

This false belief started in the early day of Reiki teachings (and is still around today) in an attempt to appeal to

---

[32] I have a DVD program I produced specifically to help with this situation entitled "How to Contact Spirits, Angels and Departed Loved Ones, A Step-by-Step Guide."

a greater populace and attract more students to Reiki classes. The message was, besides healing yourself and others with Reiki, you can also use Reiki on machines[33] such as appliances, cars, and now computers, etc. Reiki is a healing modality, not a mechanic's tool.

Reiki lineage is important

With so many Reiki Systems having different teachings and methods today, the importance of lineage is really moot. Reiki Healers today usually have a combination of lineages because they have taken Attunements from different Reiki Masters of different systems. What is important is the Reiki Healer's teachings and how they are used. In other words, what is important is the here and now.

A circle of Reiki Healers feel lineage is really an issue of prestige, of course, with their lineage being the most prestigious. They will make statements to the effect that Reiki Healers from other lineages are not trained properly or other lineages are not legitimate. This is all nonsense and ego talking. All Reiki being used today is linked to Usui Reiki in some concept, shape or form and all Reiki Systems have the same prestige in respect that Reiki helps people. Lineage might have an importance in breeding animals and dog shows, but not Reiki Healing.

---

[33] I'm sure I'll receive emails from people swearing Reiki has fixed machines in their life, and if they believed it happened, it did. My point is if Reiki is going to be taken seriously and spread into the mainstream population this belief is not needed to attract Reiki students anymore. In other words, does a Healer tell a person, "I can help you with the pain in your lower back, and by the way, bring in your broken blender and I'll heal that also." Or, perhaps, "While you're here for your headache, if your car has problems..."

Reiki always produces physical signs

Reiki does not always produce physical signs when it flows. Reiki Healers and their clients are always concerned about this. They like to have physical signs to affirm that Reiki is flowing during Reiki Attunements and treatments. It seems to be human nature to want to have physical signs to wrap the conscious mind around, to confirm Reiki.

The majority of time there are indeed physical signs when channeling and receiving Reiki, but there are times when no physical signs manifest. When this does happen with minimal or no practical indicators of Reiki flowing, ultimately the Reiki will have the same outcome as if physical signs were present.

Reiki is a subtle energy. It has to be this way to be used and absorbed as it flows into the body. If it entered the body like a charge of electricity, there would be major problems with utilizing this life force.

Here are some of the common physical sensations people experience when channeling Reiki: warm to very hot hands, tingling sensations in hands or throughout body, hands cold to ice cold, numbness in hands and/or arms. You might experience a combination of sensations or have your own unique sensations.

The person receiving the Reiki may feel the same physical signs as the Healer. Or perhaps the Healer won't feel anything, but the person receiving Reiki will, or vice versa. In terms of physical signs being present or not, each Reiki

Treatment or Attunement will produce different results and experiences.

You should see your Reiki Guides

It's a common belief that everyone has spirit guides (this term includes angels) watching over and aiding their lives. And it is taught that there will be Reiki Guides, which include higher beings, angels, spiritual ancestors, etc., working through the Healer during Reiki Healings and Attunements. The only problem with this is that some Reiki teachings imply that you should be able to see the guides and if you don't, you do not have any. To make matters worse, if you do not have any guides present, your Reiki healings will not be as strong. This is not true. Just because you cannot see Reiki Guides does not mean they are not there, because they are. Do not worry about not being able to see Reiki Guides. Your healing work will not be affected.

Reiki is different and unique from other healing energy

Reiki is the life force that keeps us alive. Once the life force is no longer flowing, our physical bodies cease to exist. All cultures have their own name for the life force or energy that is essential to our physical being. You could refer to the Chi of the Chinese culture or the Prana of the Indian culture, and you'd be talking about the same thing. There is only one universal life force no matter what name you give it. I personally call it Reiki. I believe all energy Healers use this same life force in the energy healing modality they choose to use.

What is confusing is when Reiki Healers and different schools of Reiki call *their* Reiki a special energy, different from any other life force energy, unique, more powerful, better, purer, higher vibration quality, different rays, higher levels...the list goes on. No matter what they would like you to believe about their special Reiki, the Reiki that empowers them is the same Reiki that empowers all Healers.

If a Healer promotes the attributes of their Reiki as being better than other Reiki, besides being untrue, the claim is based on hidden motives that will vary from Healer to Healer (e.g., fill classes, sell Reiki materials).

He who is contented is rich.

\- Lao Tzu

Nothing is softer or more flexible than water, yet nothing can resist it.

- Lao Tzu

False Beliefs on Reiki & Karma

FOURTEEN

Accepting money for Reiki is bad karma

Accepting a fee for Reiki is not bad karma. This false belief arises from a segment of Healers who believe that money is evil and/or healing should not be charged for and should be freely given. They also believe if they accept money for healing, it will create bad karma in their lives. As I mentioned before, nothing is ever free. There is always an exchange on some level for anything. If a Healer is giving Reiki to relatives or friends, of course there is already an exchange of love and friendship, but if a Healer is teaching or seeing clients, money can be exchanged without fear of repercussion (i.e., bad karma). The caveat is the teacher and student both should feel it is a fair exchange of time and services rendered.

Reiki Healers cannot change their karma

It's a false belief that Reiki Healers cannot change their karma once they become a Healer. If true, there would be no need for free will in a person's life. We all know that each person has free will in life and is able to implement it. The decisions and choices we make in our lives create our karma. Now a person could have a destiny to become a Reiki Healer, but that also could be changed with free will.

A Reiki Healer can create good karma and prevent bad karma by always performing positive actions coupled with positive thinking and talking. Another option for a Reiki Healer is to send Reiki in the past to help heal a situation that is causing bad karma in the present.

Healing of issues that aren't meant to be healed creates bad karma

This false belief is about Healers who perform perceived inappropriate healing and as a consequence, will create bad karma in their lives. In other words, a Reiki Healer heals a person who is not supposed to be healed because of the person's own karma or the healing is not for the person's highest good. It is also said if healings are driven by ego (the Healer's), bad karma is created. I have even heard that a Healer who attempts inappropriate healings may channel bad astral beings in lieu of Reiki Guides, which will cause bad karma.

If a person is not meant to be healed, they will not heal. There is never an inappropriate healing because nobody in this physical world has access to that information. For a healing to be called inappropriate by anyone would be passing judgment and be subjective. All a Healer needs to do is keep an open mind about the outcome of Reiki Treatments and not worry about bad karma being created. This belief has been created by Healers who are jealous of other Healers' results and is completely false.

Chujiro Hayashi's suicide has created bad karma in subsequent Reiki Attunements

Chujiro Hayashi is understood to be the last Reiki Master trained by Usui before his death, and the Reiki Master who trained and attuned Hawayo Takata. It is claimed he committed suicide to avoid being a participant in World War II.

It has been rumored that all subsequent Attunements from the Chujiro Hayashi Reiki lineage can create bad karma since he committed suicide in 1940. This is just a fear tactic to direct prospective Reiki students to different healing modality teachings or newly invented Reiki Systems. You cannot acquire another person's karma. This belief is false.

He who controls may be powerful, but he who has mastered himself is mightier still.

- Lao Tzu

False Beliefs about
Reiki & Psychic Abilities

FIFTEEN

Reiki Psychic Attunements
give you psychic abilities

The Reiki Psychic Attunement does not give you instant psychic abilities, although it appears that way with some people. If this does happen (instant psychic abilities), it's because the Attunement has revealed psychic abilities the person already had. Everyone has psychic gifts, but not everyone is aware of their gifts or explores and expands these talents.

The Psychic Attunement helps increase the psychic abilities of a person from whatever level they are at now. For example, if a person is clairvoyant, they will receive stronger, clearer messages after the Attunement. A person who receives information in dreams will experience more informative and clearer dreams.

To put it simply, the Reiki Psychic Attunement helps open and expand your natural psychic abilities by clearing your mental, spiritual, physical and emotional bodies so your psychic gifts can surface and/or expand.

After taking the Psychic Attunement you might not be consciously aware of any increase (shift) of psychic abilities, but that does not mean it is not happening. Most of the time it's a gradual, subtle shift with an accumulative effect on your psychic abilities. Your expanded awareness from the Attunement might be as straightforward as making a good decision in your life or as far reaching as seeing future events.

There is caution with this Attunement. Only receive it or give it to a client once every three to four weeks. On occasion, people will take the Attunement over and over in a brief period of time. Unfortunately, they may start receiving too much information at once and be unable to process and/or understand it, and may become unbalanced and confused. There is no great harm in this, however, because once a person stops taking the Attunement the information[34] will slow down and he or she will be able to process and understand it, and they will become balanced again. Take the Attunement sparingly and wait and see what unfolds. You can receive all other Reiki Attunements as many times as you like for reinforcement and clearing.

I have included the steps for the Reiki Psychic Attunement at the back of this book for the people who want to give it to their clients. I also have a Reiki Psychic Attunement DVD[35] program if you want to receive the Attunement yourself.

Psychic abilities are not a part of Reiki

Psychic abilities are an integral part of Reiki. The more Reiki Attunements you receive (and give), the more your psychic abilities expand, especially your intuition. I have read where the teachings of early Reiki actually encouraged the opening of a person's inner perception to help with healing.

For many the word *psychic* is associated with a negative connotation and should not be related to healing. However, being psychic is basically being aware of what's going on in your life. This includes people, places, things, events and your body and mind. It is being aware on all levels - mentally, physically, spiritually and emotionally. As these abilities increase, they will help with facilitating your own healing and that of others.

---

[34] This information can be in the form of dreams, visions, smells, numbers, déjà vu, etc.

[35] Reiki Psychic Attunement Open and Expand Your Psychic Abilities DVD.

Channeled Reiki information
is always reliable

All channeled[36] Reiki information is not always true or correct. The problem with most channeled information is that it is filtered through the receiver's bias and memory. This means, when the receiver interprets the information, it takes on the receiver's spin. Even if the claim is that a spirit is talking directly through the medium, the information goes through the human system and the spirit will use the vocabulary and memory of the conduit. It is almost impossible to change this. This means the information might come in correctly, but the outgoing message is altered. When weighing the validity of channeled information about Reiki you have to ask yourself if it makes sense, and decide if it resonates well enough with you to believe it. When you do this test you will discover most of the channeled Reiki information out there will not pass.

---

[36] Channeled used in this context does mean receiving information from the other side, spirits, Reiki Guides, etc.

At the center of your being you have the answer; you know who you are and you know what you want.

- Lao Tzu

Music in the soul can be heard by the universe.
- Lao Tzu

Reiki & Religion/Spirituality
False Beliefs

SIXTEEN

Reiki is only for spiritual people

You don't have to be a spiritually evolved or inclined person to become a Reiki Healer. Nevertheless, Reiki's concepts are spiritual in principal and do encourage spiritual growth. As you use Reiki, there is a distinct possibility that your spiritual awareness will expand. The false belief that Reiki is only for spiritual people is told by misguided Healers who personally feel Reiki is only for spiritual people and would like to it be so.

Reiki is a religion

Reiki is not a religion. Reiki teachings are not based on acceptance or practice of any religious dogma. Nor does a person need to alter any religious or spiritual beliefs held in order to become a Reiki Healer. People who are ignorant on the teachings of Reiki perpetrate this false belief. Once a person takes the time to learn about Reiki, it will be quickly understood that it is not a religion.

Christians do not use Reiki

All you have to is go to the Internet and use any popular search engine and type in "Christians and Reiki." When all the search results are returned, you will discover for yourself how false this belief is.

The number of open-minded Christians who have become Reiki Healers is growing. They have found Reiki healing useful for themselves and others and do not see it as a conflict with their Christian beliefs. Of course, there is still a large segment of Christianity that frowns upon the practice of Reiki or any other energy healing teachings other than those of Jesus Christ. As time moves on and Reiki awareness increases, I am sure Christians from this segment will become more open to Reiki and its benefits.

Reiki should not be used with other spiritual practices

A segment of Reiki Healers claim that Reiki should not be used with other spiritual practices, that Reiki should be used as a spiritual practice in and of itself. They assert that by mixing Reiki with other spiritual practices, a person's Reiki becomes diluted and is not as strong. This is usually the same group that does not want to combine Reiki with other healing modalities.

As mentioned before, Reiki can be used with any religion or spiritual practice and it will not harm its potential in healing. It is my belief it can only enhance Reiki healing if you combine it with spiritual practices of your choice.

Be content with what you have; rejoice in the way things are. When you realize there is nothing lacking, the whole world belongs to you.

\- Lao Tzu

False Beliefs in Reiki History

SEVENTEEN

Hawayo Takata's history of Reiki is true

The bulk of the Reiki history that Hawayo Takata told is false. That fact is pretty well established now by extensive research that has been published in books and articles. Nobody really knows how many, if any, of the stories were told to her and if she believed them, or if she intentionally fabricated the stories about Reiki. It is a moot point anyway, the history doesn't change what Reiki can do today.

However, it is generally accepted that her intentions in telling false stories was to create a buzz about Reiki and give it a larger-than-life history to help spread the teachings in the West. Everything happens for a reason and the false history she taught did indeed help Reiki get a foothold in the West. This in turn gave Reiki a chance to grow to where it is today in popularity. With today's generation of Healers, the embellished Reiki history is no longer needed for Reiki's survival as a healing system.

The following false beliefs are the ones that seem to still surface in spite of the fact that they have been debunked many times before in books and articles. I think the reason for this is many Reiki Masters just have not removed these false beliefs from their teachings for new Reiki Healers.

Mikao Usui was a Christian

Mikao Usui was a Buddhist, not a Christian. There is no verification of his being a minister, missionary, monk or a teacher of Christianity.

The most famous false version of Usui and Christianity is that he was teaching the Bible to a class when one of his students asked him if he could duplicate the healing of laying-on of hands by Jesus. Of course he said he could not. This question set in motion his immediate resignation from teaching. He then traveled to the United States to receive further Christian training at the University of Chicago (see the next false belief) in a quest for learning the healing powers of Jesus.

Mikao Usui studied at the University of Chicago

Many people have researched the database and documention for the time period Mikao Usui was said to have studied at the University of Chicago in an effort to substantiate the claim of his attendance. The research has shown there is no evidence that Mikao Usui ever attended that university.

Mikao Usui worked in a beggars' quarter for seven years

The false belief that Mikao Usui worked in a beggars' quarter for seven years was told by Takata. This experience led him to believe that it was necessary to receive some form of payment for healings and teachings. Although there is a possibility Usui might have worked in a beggars' quarter or something similar, it could have never been for seven years. The story did have redeeming qualities in that it taught the concepts of value for value (compensation for healing) and appreciation for that which is given.

Mikao Usui was a medical doctor

Hawayo Takata called Mikao Usui "Dr. Usui." No evidence has been revealed that verifies Mikao Usui was a medical doctor or even had a Ph.D. To further substantiate that he was not a doctor, it has been reported there is no mention of him being a doctor on his memorial stone in Japan. To give Takata the benefit of doubt on this false story, she may have used "doctor" as a Western interpretation for Sensei[37], as he was called in Japan.

Hawayo Takata revived the dead

A story is told about how Takata felt compelled to give Reiki to a friend's corpse about half an hour after the friend had died. Takata channeled Reiki to the woman's heart and she miraculously came back to life just before a coffin was brought into the room, in which they meant to place her body. The woman lived another five years. There is no documentation of this miracle ever happening, it's just hearsay. This false belief did help build up Takata's status as a Healer and thus helped her find clients and students.

Reiki evolved from Japan

The modern day practice of Reiki was rediscovered in Japan. That rediscovery and rebirth of Reiki has evolved into the Reiki teachings used today, but Reiki's early roots and concepts evolved from China.

Huang Ti Nei Ching Su Wen or the Yellow Emperor's classic (called Nei Ching for short) was the first important text on Chinese medicine written around 2674 B.C. In the Nei Ching, ki is described as the Universal Energy that nourishes and sustains all life forms. It explained that ki flows through the universe and every living organism. The Nei Ching taught the non-restricted flow of ki in the

---

[37] Sensei is a title of respect given by a student to a teacher in Japan.

body allows a person to remain healthy, while a restricted or blocked flow of ki in the body leads to disease. This is the same principal used in Reiki today.

These teachings from the Nei Ching where blended into Buddhist and other teachings and migrated from China to Korea and to Japan in about the seventh century. That modern Reiki evolved from Japan would be a true belief.

Reiki Psychic Attunement

The following are the step-by-step instructions for performing the Reiki Psychic Attunement. If you use non-traditional Reiki Symbols that are the equivalent of the Reiki traditional Master, Power and Long Distance Symbols you can use them in place of the traditional Reiki Symbols in the Psychic Attunement.

There are three parts to the Attunement. With the Psychic Attunement you will be working with the Crown Chakra and Sixth Chakra (third eye). The person receiving the Attunement rests his or her hands in their lap. You prepare the same way for this Attunement as with the other Reiki Attunements, except your intent is to give a Psychic Attunement.

It is worth mentioning again. Only receive the Attunement or give it to a client or student once every three to four weeks. Any questions on this please review Chapter 15 the false belief "Reiki Psychic Attunements give you psychic abilities" before you proceed with an Attunement.

Reiki Psychic Attunement

1st Part from the back

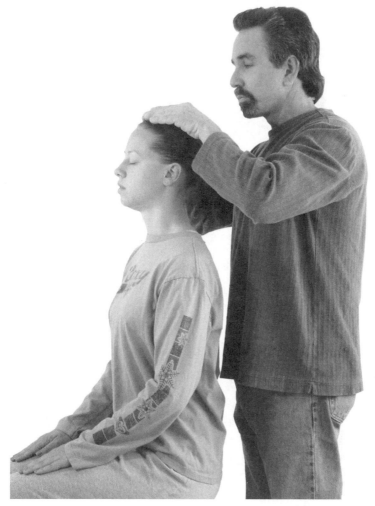

1. I place both hands on top of the head, meditating for 15 to 30 seconds to start the Reiki connection with the person.

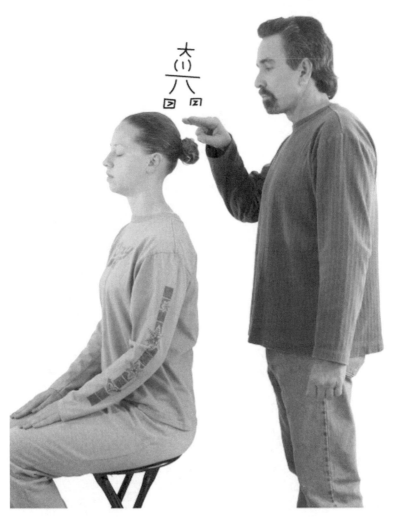

2. I draw the Master Symbol in the air at the back of the head and I visualize it going into the back of the head stopping in the middle. While this is being done, the symbol's name is said silently one time.

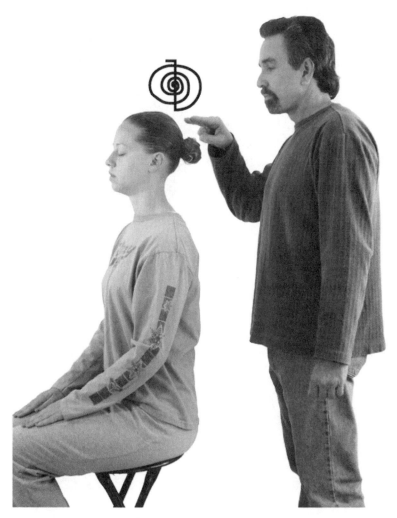

3. I draw the Power Symbol in the air at the back
of the head and I visualize it going into the back
of the head stopping in the middle. While this is
being done, the symbol's name is said silently
one time.

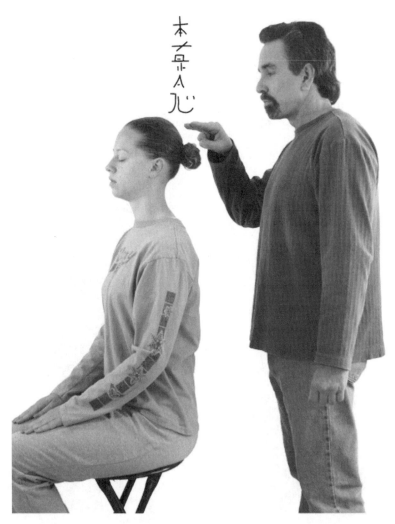

4. I draw the Long Distance Symbol in the air
at the back of the head and I visualize it going
into the back of the head stopping in the middle.
While this is being done, the symbol's name is
said silently one time.

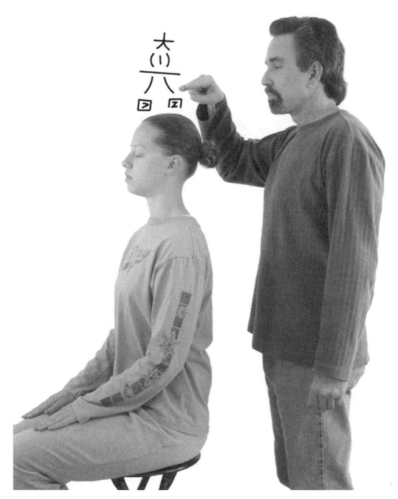

5. I draw the Master Symbol on top of the Crown Chakra and visualize it going into the top of the head stopping in the middle. While this is being done, the symbol's name is said silently one time.

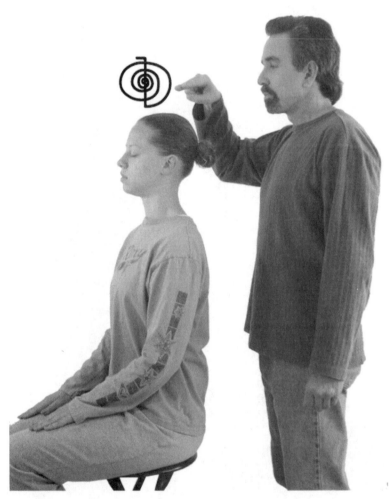

6. I draw the Power Symbol on top of the Crown Chakra and visualize it going into the top of the head stopping in the middle. While this is being done, the symbol's name is said silently one time.

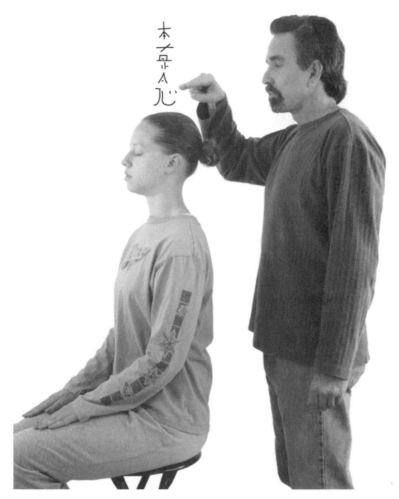

7. I draw the Long Distance Symbol on top of the Crown Chakra and visualize it going into the top of the head stopping in the middle. While this is being done, the symbol's name is said silently one time.

2nd Part from the front

1. I step to the front of the person.

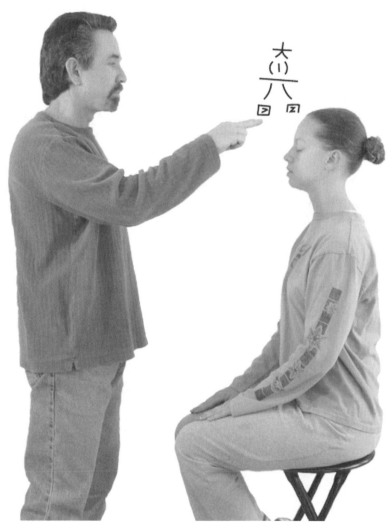

2. I draw the Master Symbol in front of the Sixth Chakra in the air and visualize it going into the third eye, stopping in the middle of the head. While this is being done, the symbol's name is said silently one time.

169

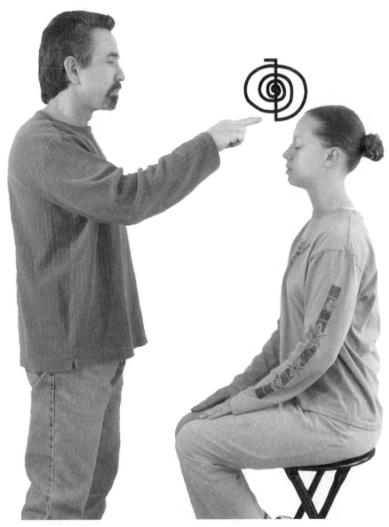

3. I draw the Power Symbol in front of the Sixth Chakra in the air and visualize it going into the third eye, stopping in the middle of the head. While this is being done, the symbol's name is said silently one time.

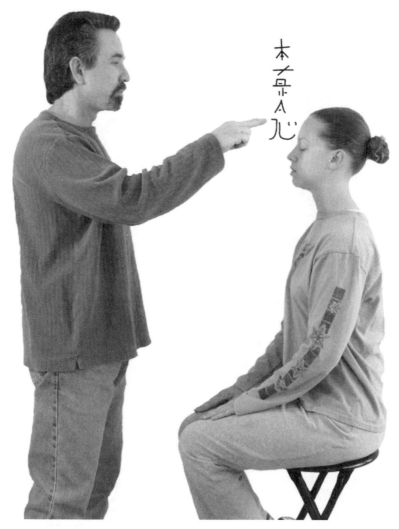

4. I draw the Long Distance Symbol in front of the Sixth Chakra in the air and visualize it going into the third eye, stopping in the middle of the head. While this is being done, the symbol's name is said silently one time.

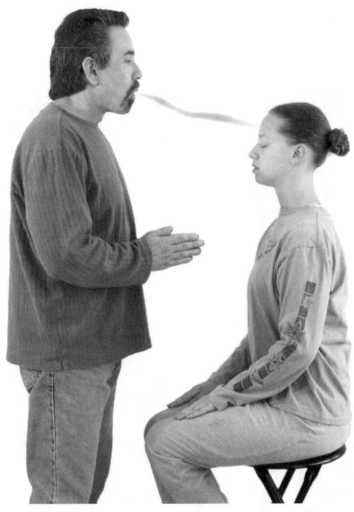

5. Then, I lightly blow on the Sixth Chakra for a few seconds, and at the same time hold the intent that I am clearing and releasing any blockages in the Sixth Chakra.

3rd Part from the back

1. I go to the back of the person.

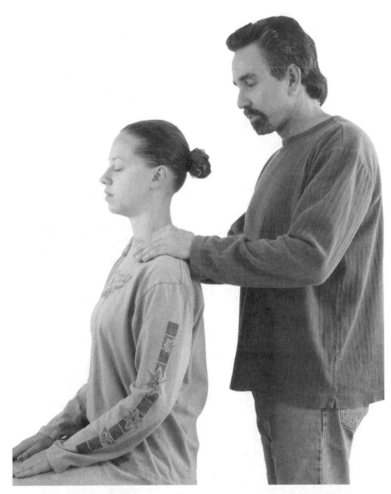

2. I place my hands on the shoulders and look
down into the Crown Chakra, visualizing into
the middle of the head, stopping where the
Sixth Chakra comes straight across. I place a silent
affirmation into that area three times. The
affirmation is, "This person's psychic abilities are
now fully opened."

174

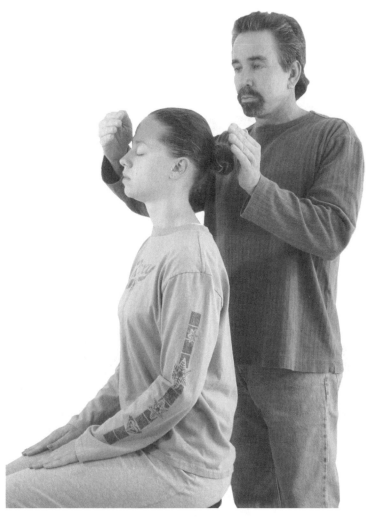

3. I then place one hand on the Sixth Chakra, and the other on the back of the head. I state silently, "I now seal this process with Divine love and wisdom." I keep my hands in that position for several minutes and channel Reiki.

175

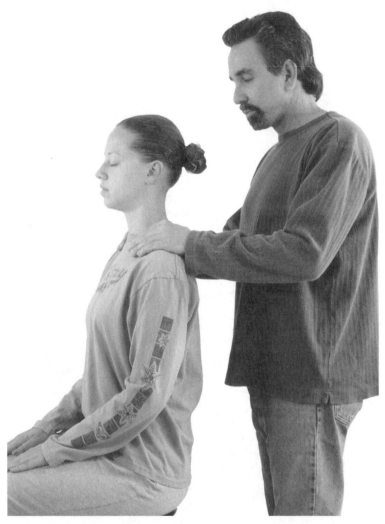

4. I place my hands on the shoulders and give a blessing which is, "We are both blessed by this process."

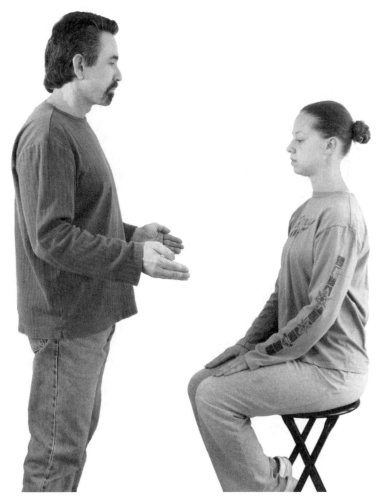

5. I move to the front, and then ask the person to breethe deeply and slowly while opening their eyes.

The Reiki Psychic Attunement is complete.

Reiki Mandala

The Reiki Mandala can be used for healing, meditation, and to help with your intent in Long Distance Healing. Feel free to make a copy for your personal use.

Reiki Mental/Emotional Symbol Illustrations

Symbol 33
Sei He Ki

Symbol 34
Sei He Ki

Symbol 35
Sei He Ki

Symbol 36
Sei He Ki

Reiki Mental/Emotional Symbol Illustrations

Symbol 37
Sei He Ki

Symbol 38
Sei He Ki

Symbol 39
Sei He Ki

Symbol 40
Sei He Ki

Reiki Mental/Emotional Symbol Illustrations

Symbol 41
Sei He Ki

Symbol 42
Sei He Ki

Symbol 43
Sei He Ki

Symbol 44
Sei He Ki

Reiki Mental/Emotional Symbol Illustrations

Symbol 45
Sei He Ki

Symbol 46
Sei He Ki

Symbol 47
Sei He Ki

Symbol 48
Sei He Ki

Continued From Page 78

Reiki Long Distance Symbol Illustrations

Symbol 49
Hon Sha Ze Sho Nen

Symbol 50
Hon Sha Ze Sho Nen

Symbol 51
Hon Sha Ze Sho Nen

Symbol 52
Hon Sha Ze Sho Nen

Reiki Long Distance Symbol Illustrations

Symbol 53
Hon Sha Ze Sho Nen

Symbol 54
Hon Sha Ze Sho Nen

Symbol 55
Hon Sha Ze Sho Nen

Symbol 56
Hon Sha Ze Sho Nen

Reiki Long Distance Symbol Illustrations

Symbol 57
Hon Sha Ze Sho Nen

Symbol 58
Hon Sha Ze Sho Nen

Symbol 59
Hon Sha Ze Sho Nen

Symbol 60
Hon Sha Ze Sho Nen

Reiki Long Distance Symbol Illustrations

Symbol 61
Hon Sha Ze Sho Nen

Symbol 62
Hon Sha Ze Sho Nen

Symbol 63
Hon Sha Ze Sho Nen

Symbol 64
Hon Sha Ze Sho Nen

Reiki Master Symbol Illustrations

Symbol 65
Dai Koo Myo

Symbol 66
Dai Koo Myo

Symbol 67
Dai Koo Myo

Symbol 68
Dai Koo Myo

Reiki Master Symbol Illustrations

Symbol 69
Dai Koo Myo

Symbol 70
Dai Koo Myo

Symbol 71
Dai Koo Myo

Symbol 72
Dai Koo Myo

Non-traditional Symbols

Symbol 73 Elohim. This symbol is depicted by itself or side by side like in the illustration. Its intent is hope.

Symbol 74 & 74b Eeftchay or Eeeftchay. There are two versions illustrated. The intent here is for spiritual guidance from the 'Higher Self.'

Symbol 75 & 75b Fire Serpent. There are two versions illustrated. The intent for this symbol is to ground energy in the lower Chakras, or thrust energy upwards into the higher Chakras. It can also be used to connect all Chakras when receiving an Attunement.

Symbol 76 Johre. A multi-tasking symbol. Its intent is to release blockages and to provide peace, protection, balance and success.

Symbol 77 & 77b Om. There are two versions illustrated. This symbol's intent is to purify and protect a person. It can be used in Attunements to seal in symbols.

Symbol 78 Rama. The intent for this symbol is to clear our lower six Chakras of negative energy.

Symbol 79 Raku Bolt or Raku. This symbol's intent is to disconnect or ground and seal in symbol(s) and energies at the end of an Attunement or treatment.

Symbol 80 Tamarasha or Tama. The intent for this symbol is to unblock Chakras. It may also be used to reduce pain.

Non-traditional Symbols

Symbol 81, 81b, 81c, 81d, 81e Master Symbol (aka Dai Koo Myo). Symbols can have different names and are used in different Reiki Systems with similar, if not the same intent as the traditional Reiki Master Symbol

Symbol 82 Kriya. This symbol's intent is to balance the physical body or to convert thoughts into achievements.

Symbol 83, 83b, 83c, 83d, 83e Power Symbol. Symbols can have different names and are used in different Reiki Systems with similar, if not the same intent as the traditional Reiki Power Symbol.

Symbol 84 Sei He Ki. The intent is similar if not the same as the traditional Reiki Mental/Emotional Symbol.

Symbol 85 Yin-Yang Balance. This symbol's intent is to balance male and female energies.

Symbol 86 Hi Lo God Alignment. This symbol's intent is to align you with your source (God).

Symbol 87 Mer Ka Fa Ka Lish Ma. This symbol is used to activate dormant DNA.

Symbol 88 Angel Wings. The intent of this symbol is to fulfill your potential on all levels (physical, mental, emotional and spiritual).

Symbol 89 Fire Clover. This symbol's intent is to heal emotional issues of the heart and/or sexual issues.

Non-traditional Symbol Illustrations

Symbol 73
Elohim

Symbol 74
Eeftchay

Symbol 74B
Eeeftchay

Symbol 75
Fire Serpent

Non-traditional Symbol Illustrations

Symbol 75b
Fire Serpent

Symbol 76
Johre

Symbol 77
Om

Symbol 77b
Om

Non-traditional Symbol Illustrations

Symbol 78
Rama

Symbol 79
Raku Bolt

Symbol 80
Tamarasha

Symbol 81
Master Symbol

Non-traditional Symbol Illustrations

Symbol 81b
Master Symbol

Symbol 81c
Master Symbol

Symbol 81d
Master Symbol

Symbol 81e
Master Symbol

Non-traditional Symbol Illustrations

Symbol 82
Kriya

Symbol 83
Power Symbol

Symbol 83b
Power Symbol

Symbol 83c
Power Symbol

Non-traditional Symbol Illustrations

Symbol 83d
Power Symbol

Symbol 83e
Power Symbol

Symbol 84
Sei He Ki

Symbol 85
Yin-Yang Balance

Non-traditional Symbol Illustrations

Symbol 86
Hi Lo God Alignment

Symbol 87
Mer Ka Fa Ka Lish Ma

Symbol 88
Angel Wings

Symbol 89
Fire Clover

Index

Selected Bibliography

Baginski, B. & Sharamon, S. *Reiki Universal Life Energy.* LifeRythm. 1985 ISBN 0-940795-02-7

Borang, K. *Principles of Reiki.* Thorsons.1997 ISBN 0-7225-3406-X

Brown, F. *Living Reiki Takata's Teachings.* LifeRythm. 1992 ISBN 0-940795-10-8

Haberky, H. *Hawayo Takata's Story.* Archedigm Publications. 1990 ISBN 0-944135-06-04

Morris, J. *Reiki Hands That Heal.* 1996 ISBN 1888196-05-X

Nevius, S. & Arnold L. *The Reiki Handbook* PSI Press.1982 ISBN 0-9625500-1-9

Paul, Nina. *Reiki for Dummies.* Wiley Publishing. 2006 ISBN 0-7645-9907-0

Petter, F. *The Original Reiki Handbook of Dr. Mikao Usui.* Lotus Press. 1999 ISBN 0-914955-57-8

Petter, F. *Reiki Fire.* Lotus Press. 1997 ISBN 0-914955-5-0

Slate, J., *Aura Energy For Health, Healing & Balance* Llewellyn Publications. 1999 ISBN 1-567186378

Steine, Bronwen and Stiene, Frans. *The Reiki Source Book.* Oriental Press. 2003 ISBN 1-903816-55-6

HOW TO ORDER DVDS, CDs, BOOKS

To buy any of the following Books, DVDs or CDs, check with your local bookstore, or www.healingreiki.com, or email bodymindheal@aol.com, or call 949-263-4676

DVDs-CDs-BOOKS

BOOKS by STEVE MURRAY

Reiki The Ultimate Guide
Learn Sacred Symbols and Attunements
Plus Reiki Secrets You Should Know

Reiki The Ultimate Guide Vol. 2
Learn Reiki Healing with Chakras
plus New Reiki Healing Attunements
for All Levels

Reiki The Ultimate Guide Vol. 3
Learn New Reiki Aura Attunements
Heal Mental and Emotional Issues

Cancer Guided Imagery Program
For Radiation, Chemotherapy, Surgery
and Recovery

Stop Eating Junk!
In 5 Minutes a Day for 21 Days

Reiki False Beliefs Exposed for All
Misinformation Kept Secret By A
Few Revealed

DVDS by STEVE MURRAY

Reiki Master Attunement
Become a Reiki Master

Reiki 1st Level Attunement
Give Healing Energy to Yourself
and Others

Reiki 2nd Level Attunement
Learn and Use the Reiki Sacred
Symbols

Reiki Psychic Attunement
Open and Expand Your Psychic
Abilities

Reiki Healing Attunement
Heal Emotional-Mental Physical-
Spiritual Issues

Lose Fat and Weight
Stop Eating Junk!
In 5 Minutes a Day for 21 Days

Cancer Guided Imagery
Program for Radiation

Cancer Guided Imagery
Program for Chemotherapy

Cancer Guided Imagery
Program for Surgery

30-Day Subliminal
Weight Loss Program

Pain Relief Using Your
Unconscious Mind
A Subliminal Program

Fear & Stress Relief
Using Your Unconscious Mind
A Subliminal Program

Stop Smoking Using Your
Unconscious Mind
A Subliminal Program

CDs by STEVE MURRAY

Reiki Healing Music
Attunement: Volume One

Reiki Healing Music
Attunement: Volume Two

Reiki Psychic Music
Attunement: Volume One

Reiki Psychic Music
Attunement: Volume Two

Cancer Fear & Stress Relief Program
Reduce Fear and Stress During Cancer
Treatment and Recovery

DVDs by BODY & MIND PRODUCTIONS

Learning to Read the Tarot
Intuitively

Learning to Read the Symbolism
of the Tarot

More of what people are saying ...

The third book in Steve's Reiki Guide series, Reiki, The Ultimate Guide, Learn New Reiki Aura Attunements, is the most indispensable book I have encountered in quite a long time. Most everyone we know has numerous mental and emotional problems, some bigger than others, all of which can be healed through the techniques taught in this book. Imagine having the ability to channel the energy needed to help someone stop smoking, end depression, lose weight, or heal his or her anger. Healing all of these and many more illnesses are taught in this book - the most definitive book on healing emotional & mental issues with Reiki that I have ever seen! *ST*

Reiki, The Ultimate Guide Vol.2 makes a great resource for continued Reiki practicing. It's loaded with great info. I found the explanations of Meridians and Chakras very interesting. Lots of added drawings, including one outlining the Meridians as well as a Chakra Formula Chart and the easy-to-follow Healing Attunement pictorials and step-by-step instructions for all levels. By the end of the book, you're all ready to carry out Healing Attunements on your clients to enhance their Reiki experience. A great book to complement any Reiki Healer's library. *SC*

I have both of Steve's previous works and acquired this one as a first edition. Steve's style is beautifully simplistic. He gives in-depth details on the subject and presents the subject in a way that all can benefit from Reiki. If you want to know about Reiki, then this is the author you need to seek out. I have read works by other authors who add nothing to the subject, nor do they give information or symbols of Reiki or indeed how to get the most from it. This man does. He has brought the gift to all who would like to share in it. Definitely worth having on your bookshelf. *PW*

I have now purchased your three books and four DVDs, all of which are concise and to the point. The books make Reiki as I think it should be - available to everyone who is interested and not surrounded by secrecy that still appears to be present in some areas and with certain Masters. The DVDs are excellent and I find them as good as a personal attunement. *DS*

In Steve's new book, the pages are packed with diagrams for all healing attunements, ranging from addictions to stress. This no doubt is Steve's most powerful book yet and is useful to anyone interested in the natural healing process. Thanks again, Steve! *BM*

I gave an attunement to a lady who is so incredibly psychic it blows my mind. I did it long distance first, then planned on doing it in person at our art show the next day. As I held my hands in front of her face, she said the energy coming from my hands was so incredibly strong that she almost had to back away. All I am saying is that it works beyond a doubt. Being an artist and potter, I have always been a "just do it" kind of person and I will believe it when I see it. Your system works fine. Just thought you might want to hear it one more time. *JT*

I have read the book and I am amazed that Mr. Murray is able to use simple and effective language to deliver the Reiki message. He makes it quite clear that Reiki can be used by anyone and is useful for everyday life, not limited to the Reiki masters of the Orient. Everyone can benefit from this book. *PR*

I have been trying and trying to find a Reiki Master to learn from for a little over two years. The prices were outrageous ($250 for first and second level, $10,000 for Master level), and I read on many sites that the "energy exchange" of this much money was to be sure that the student was "sincere." I am very sincere about my desire to learn and share Reiki, but do not have that kind of money to "prove" my sincerity. I became disheartened by all of that and had almost given up on ever being able to learn because the cost was way out of my reach, then I found Steve Murray's books and DVDs. I received Steve Murray's Reiki 1, 2, and Master level DVDs and his 1st, 2nd, and 3rd books as a gift. I highly recommend Steve's books and DVDs. His books are very easy to read, really hard to put down, and will be great to refer back to anytime. The DVDs are very meditative and powerful too! I will be using them for re-attunements as needed. Thank you again for everything, Steve! Keep up the great work you are doing! *KS*

Reiki Grid

The Reiki Grid is a tool that has many uses. My students like to use it to help focus and use their intent, especially when they are new to distant healing. There are many grids, complex to simple, and all will work. I have this particular Reiki Grid (Photo 1) made for my students. It is a 10"x10" glass engraved grid with the flower of life, and it comes with a felt mat diagram for suggested stone placement and the following stones:

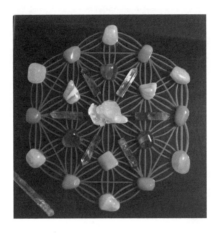

(6) Angelite for dispelling fear, anger, and encouraging forgiveness. It is also used to connect with spirit guides, the higher self, and guardian angels.
(6) Rose Quartz for unconditional love and to bring gentleness, forgiveness, and tolerance.
(3) Blue Lace Agate for assisting in flight, grace, reaching higher Spiritual planes, and communicating with Angels.
(3) Amethyst for stability, peace, calmness, and balance. It engenders courage, inner strength and spirit communication.
(6) Polished Fluorite points for promoting spiritual and psychic wholeness and development, truth, protection, and peace.
(1) Natural Quartz Cluster for your center/cap stone. It is a power stone that harmonizes and balances. It enhances energy and thoughts, and purifies the spiritual, mental, and physical bodies.
(1) Natural Quartz Laser Crystal to activate your grid.

More information on the Reiki Grid on my web site.

About the Author

Steve Murray is the author of the best selling **Reiki The Ultimate Guide** trilogy and has a series of self-healing programs on DVD. The DVD subjects include Reiki Attunements, Cancer Guided Imagery, weight loss, pain, fear, and stress relief, just to name a few. He has produced four Reiki CDs for healing, meditation and psychic work.

Steve is an experienced Usui Reiki Master, but one of his most powerful Attunements came from the High Priest of the Essene Church, which made him an Essene Healer. The Essenes have been healers for more than 2,000 years. Steve is also a Hypnotherapist and a member of the National League of Medical Hypnotherapists and National Guild of Hypnotists.

"Shanti" **Steve Murray**